Color**STRUCK**

—————— Uzoma Uponi ——————

ISBN 978-1-63903-891-6 (paperback)
ISBN 978-1-63903-892-3 (digital)

Christian Faith Publishing, Inc.
832 Park Avenue
Meadville, PA 16335
www.christianfaithpublishing.com

Printed in the United States of America

This book is dedicated to Queen Henry-Okafor, Coletta Haskin, Charity (Njoku) Akaeze, Joan Duru, and Chinwe Elendu—beloved sisters and prayer partners, who labored with me to bring this story to birth. Chinwe Elendu now lives in the full presence of Jesus and continues to cheer us on.

—— ACKNOWLEDGMENTS ——

Thank you, Matthew, for your kindness and support as I wrote this book. You continue to be a godly role model to our boys and to me.

Thank you, Dede Brushaber, for reading through the manuscript with a red pen to ensure I could present a perfect copy for publication. It has been a blessing to have you and Pastor Paul at Bethany Chapel, Calgary.

Special thanks to all my readers (yes, you) for picking up this book to read. Without you, I would not have written one line. You are a blessing to me, and I hope you enjoy this story.

If storm-clouds gather darkly 'round,
And even if the heavens seem brass, without a sound,
He hears each prayer and even notes the sparrow's fall.
—C. G. Trumbull

CHAPTER 1

You don't need a reason to help your family.

—African proverb

Afam Izuwa turned right at the tarred road leading to his home in Rumuodolla residential area and breathed a sigh of relief. He had finally escaped the bustling streets of Port Harcourt City. To him, successfully maneuvering between deep potholes, rickety taxis, *okada* motorcycles, and *kekenapepe* tricycles, through packed street markets and a myriad of vendors hurling everything from newspapers to electronics in the face of every motorist and every pedestrian, was always a huge achievement.

Downshifting, he decelerated around a curve, and his compound came into view. His compound partially came into view, that is—because only the top of the house could be seen above the ten feet of concrete and four feet of wire fence that surrounded it. If the fence didn't exist, passersby would be impressed with the burnt brick property which boasted both a concrete courtyard and a colorful garden. They would see the connecting domestic quarters with its wraparound porch and towers. Because of the fence, however, all that anyone could see of the building from outside were the huge square pillars that rose to the roof and the large windows that framed the house.

He slowed down before coming to a complete stop behind the huge wrought iron gate and waited for the gateman to roll it open.

"Welcome, sir!" Musa waved as Afam slowly drove through the gate. He acknowledged the greeting with a nod and noticed but ignored the curious eyes of the group of people in the gatehouse. Probably members of the *mai-guard*'s family, he thought.

A quick shower and a bottle of cold water later, Afam took his laptop to the balcony off his bedroom to surf the internet. From where he sat, he had an unrestricted view of the buildings in Rumuodolla residential estate. The houses were on huge lots and their exclusive designs were an architect's delight. Even the high fences with their barbed wires and surveillance cameras seemed to exude a peculiar charm of their own.

His house was big, all of four thousand square feet, but the land on which it stood was bigger, making the house appear small. Half of the upper floor boasted a huge master bedroom, a study, and a balcony with panoramic views of Port Harcourt City. The other half had two large bedrooms that were used by members of his family whenever they visited. The lower level had a custom-designed kitchen and dining, a vaulted sitting room, two guest rooms, a library, and an entrance hall. There was a second balcony on the lower level that led to terraced concrete steps that zigzagged their way to the circular garden in the front yard.

Afam was not five minutes into the news headlines of the *Punch* newspaper before he heard shouting from the security gate. He recognized Musa's voice. The second belonged to a woman, and the two appeared to be arguing. He tried to ignore them, wondering which part of "I don't want to be disturbed" his security man had not understood. "No visitors," he had told all his house staff. "I don't want anybody to know I am at home for the next four weeks." That was only three days ago and now this loud ruckus at—he glanced at his watch—ten o'clock on a Saturday morning! If they didn't stop arguing soon, his gateman was going to be in big trouble with him.

"I'm sorry to disturb you, sir," Amadi's voice broke into his thoughts. Afam hadn't heard his manservant come in. "There's a family at the gate, sir. They want to see you."

He squeezed his shoulder blades together to ease the rising tension, let out a deep breath, and shook his head. Amadi looked uncomfortable but did not attempt to leave.

When the seconds turned into minutes, the servant cleared his throat and continued quietly. "I'm sorry, sir. I know you don't want to see any visitors today, but I think you should see these people."

Slightly irritated, Afam finally looked up. "This had better be an emergency, Amadi. Who are they? Do I know them?"

"A woman and three children, sir."

"What do you mean 'a woman and three children'?" Impatience laced his words. "Who are they? What are their names? What do they want with me? I don't know any 'woman and three children.'"

"The woman said her name is…" Amadi looked down to read from the open notebook in his hand. "She said her name is Binta, and that she has a message for you from your sister"—he read again from the paper—"from Mrs. Ogugua Garuba. Musa has turned her away two times this morning, but she is adamant that she must see you."

Afam froze, his eyes moving slowly from his laptop to narrow upon the servant. "From…Ogugua?" he repeated sceptically. "Where is she, this woman?"

"At the gatehouse, sir. She says it is important that she sees you. I even told her that you don't have a sister called Ogugua Garuba. I know your siblings, sir, and none of them is called Ogugua Garuba."

Afam shut his eyes, breathing in deeply and exhaling as he opened them again. He leaned back on his chair and shook his head at Amadi. "Ogugua is my half sister."

"Your what?"

"My half sister."

"Oh!" Amadi exclaimed, looking confused, but Afam didn't provide any more explanation.

"Did you say, *three* children?"

"Yes, sir, two boys and a little girl."

"Show them into the sitting room. I'll be down shortly."

The servant eyed him warily before turning away. "Yes, sir."

The last time Afam saw Ogugua was six years ago at their father's funeral. She had participated in the funeral rites, dancing when required and pouring sand in the grave at the appropriate time. She had stayed back after the burial only long enough to confirm that her father had not mentioned her in his will. Land, monetary, and property provisions had been made for Afam, for his brother, his sister, and their mother, but there had been no mention of his half sister in the will. Without any fuss or complaint, Ogugua had departed from the village in her rented vehicle afterward, leaving no contact address.

Afam clenched and unclenched his fingers. Having deliberately kept away from the family all these years, what could be prompting Ogugua to contact him now? And why him? Why not his mother or sister? He ran his palm across his forehead as nervous tension flowed over his heart. *Perhaps she has fallen into financial hardship*, he thought. He would be glad to help if indeed that was the case, but somehow, he doubted it. The Ogugua he knew would have to be on her deathbed to ask anybody in their family for help, and perhaps not even then.

He logged off from the internet and closed the laptop. In all his thirty-two years, this would be the first time his half sister had attempted to contact him.

It did not feel right.

*****

The woman waiting in the sitting room was dark in complexion. Afam thought he had never seen anyone so dark, and she looked even darker in her dark blue wrapper and matching blouse. Her braided hair was packed in a pile on her head, and a black shawl was wrapped around her neck. She was looking intently at and speaking quietly to a young child whose arms were wound tightly around her neck. Afam saw the polite awe in the faces of the two boys sitting beside her as they stared at the vaulted ceiling of the sitting room and examined the paintings on the walls. They had luggage with them—suitcases and backpacks—causing him to stop and wonder again exactly what the visit was about. Hopefully, Ogugua had not sent this woman and her children to him for help with accommodation in Port Harcourt. He would have no option but to send them away immediately if that was the case.

The instant they registered his presence, everybody rose to their feet and stared as he quickly descended the final steps.

"I'm Afam Izuwa," he said, putting his hand out to shake the woman's and going straight to the point. "I understand my sister sent you to me."

She was young, he surmised, not more than twenty-five or twenty-six. Large brown eyes contrasted with dark skin as she pressed her lips together and shook his hand. Afam could not decide if those eyes were reproachful, angry, or polite, as they returned his gaze; or if the slight tightening of her lips was a struggle to control her emotions. When a solitary tear silently raced down her cheek, his brows rose slightly. He watched her hastily wipe it away with her shawl. Had the exchange with his *mai-guard* been that terrible?

"Please sit down," he directed more gently. "What can I do for you?"

"I'm sorry, sir," she whispered through trembling lips. Another tear dribbled down her face, and she wiped it off with her shawl again. "I'm sorry." She sniffed. More tears. "Please excuse me. My name is Binta Garuba. Your…your sister was married to my brother."

His brows rose higher. What did she mean, *was* married to her brother? Weren't they still married? He withheld himself from asking, not willing to add to her emotional distress. She would probably explain her choice of words in the course of their meeting.

"I…um…the children and I have been on the road for two days now. We left Maiduguri two nights ago," she sucked in a deep breath and wiped away more tears. "Please excuse me…"

Giving her time to recover, he turned to study the children. The boys looked back at him calmly, but he could see that they too looked upset. Tears shimmered in their eyes, and the younger of the two boys rubbed his left palm across his nostrils to halt the beginnings of a runny nose.

A strange foreboding was creeping slowly up his chest as Afam waited for the woman to stop hiccupping and sniffing into her clothes. Amadi, bless him, appeared in the doorway with a pitcher of water and several glasses, which he set on the center table. He poured the water into the glasses and started to leave the room, but Afam gestured for him to stay. He did not know what news this woman bore from Ogugua, but it didn't look good, and he wanted someone else present as he heard her out.

Binta Garuba took a sip from the glass of water Amadi poured for her and nodded her thanks. She took a deep breath and started again, addressing Afam with determination. "If it's okay with you, can we speak privately? Maybe the children can stay outside while you and I talk?"

"No!" the child in her arms screamed, lifting her head to stare in horror at Binta, then covered her mouth and sank deeper into the woman's shoulder again when her gaze clashed with Afam's. His breath caught in his throat. The child was an albino—a scared and terrified albino girl. Tears were streaming down her red face, and her thick lips were trembling uncontrollably. Something in the huge eyes behind the thick glasses reminded him of a terrified kitten. Frowning, he nodded to Amadi who motioned for the children to follow him. It was hard to prise the screaming girl from Binta, but the young woman spoke gently into her ears and set her firmly on her feet, and the older boy took her hand and followed Amadi out of the living room.

As soon as they were out of earshot, Binta turned to Afam and continued in a quiet voice. "Please accept my apologies again, sir. I didn't mean to embarrass you with my tears, but the past weeks have been difficult. It's as if we had been on the road forever, trying to get to Port Harcourt, only to be chased away by your *mai-guard* when we arrived. He wouldn't let us see you. We had almost given up hope before the other man said we can come in and wait. Thank you for your time, sir."

"Well, I must take responsibility for my gateman," he replied. "I left instruction that I was not to be disturbed."

She nodded. "That's what he said."

He was anxious to know why she had come in the first place, and, *who were those children?*

"Amadi said you had a message from my sister. How is Ogugua? Is she okay?"

Binta shook her head and hung her head. Tears shimmered on her eyelashes again. She took another sip of water from the glass and swallowed hard as Afam continued to wait, warding off the ominous possibility that lay coiled like a deadly snake on the pathway of his mind.

"No," she responded finally, sucking in a deep hiccup. "Your sister is not okay. I'm sorry to be the one to tell you this, but your sister, Ogugua…and her husband, my brother, Dan… they are dead."

"What?"

"Four weeks ago."

"What did you say?" Afam held his breath.

"They're gone, sir. I'm sorry."

His breath quickened as an emotion he could not understand gripped his heart, and he felt goosebumps break out on his skin. He was not close to his sister, but he hadn't expected this. She was not even forty years old. How could she just…die?

"What happened? Was there an accident? How could they both be dead?"

"They were in Maiduguri for the Northern Nigeria Secondary Schools Quiz Challenge. Boko Haram struck at midnight and burnt down the hotel where they were lodging. Some of the guests managed to escape, but Sister Ogugua and Brother Dan didn't make it out in time."

"Oh no!" Afam cried, his heart going cold even as more goosebumps washed over him.

"I'm so sorry," her voice broke again, and she burst into fresh tears, this time covering her face with both hands and sobbing uncontrollably.

The guilt he always felt at the remembrance of his half sister came rushing through Afam's mind again. Ogugua's mother had died giving birth to her, and her father had remarried three years later. Afam had been born one year after the marriage, and although he was four years younger, he still remembered the emotional abuse his half sister had suffered in his mother's hands. Too clever to be seen physically hitting her stepdaughter, Phidelia Izuwa had not been as discrete about the neglect she had subjected the little girl to. His mother had done everything she could to push the girl toward her maternal grandmother, who had died shortly before Ogugua graduated from university.

"Just as I was at my wit's end," Binta Garuba continued, "wondering what to do with her children, I found your address among her stuff, and I knew I had to bring them to you. Peter is thirteen, John is twelve, and Kamdi is eight years old."

Afam exhaled slowly and reminded himself to breathe in again. Maybe he hadn't heard her right. "What do you mean you had to bring them to me?"

"My brother Dan and I were orphans. Sister Ogugua and the children were all the family we had. Now that they are both gone, I can't afford even the rent for our apartment, let alone the cost of school and day care. That is why I was relieved when I found your address. You and your family are my only hope now. Bringing them to you is better than sending the children to an orphanage."

Afam shook his head slowly. Too many things were happening too quickly, and he had to do something before they got out of hand. She really expected him to take in these children.

"I'm afraid you have had a wasted journey, Miss Garuba. I cannot keep the children. I am not married. I have a business to run, and I'm practically never home. If it is money you want, I can certainly contribute to the children's upkeep, within reason of course, but to have them live with me is impossible."

Binta's eyes turned to him again, and her hands lifted in supplication. "Ah, Mr. Izuwa, you don't know how much I wish I could look after them myself," she cried, shaking her head. "You don't know how much I wish I could take you up on that offer. You don't know the pain I feel at the prospect of being separated from them."

"Then why—"

"Because I'm leaving the country, that's why. I'm leaving for Scotland for my graduate studies next weekend. My brother paid for everything before his death, including my flight ticket. I don't have any job or anything to do here. This is an opportunity I don't want to miss."

Afam stared at her, aghast. Misgivings over his relationship with Ogugua or not, there was no way he was getting involved in this. Binta Garuba's brother having already paid for her graduate studies or her having to miss the opportunity to study abroad had nothing to do with him. All he knew was that she could not leave the children with him.

"I'm sorry I can't keep them," he repeated firmly. "It's totally out of the question. Couldn't you defer your education?"

He regretted the question as soon as the words left his mouth. Some things were best left unsaid.

"They are also your relations, sir," she reminded him courageously.

He acknowledged the unspoken reasoning behind the reminder. *Why would she be the one to sacrifice her dreams to look after their nephews and niece?* Afam's left foot began to beat an agitated tattoo on the carpeted floor. He knew it did not sound fair to her, but neither was the option of leaving them with him.

His thoughts drifted again as recollections of his half sister flooded his mind. Ogugua had come back from National Youth Service with a Hausa boy and an engagement ring, much to their father's fury and his mother's delight. After persuading their father to accept the wine and bride price from Ogugua's suitor, his mother had spent the years after making sure that Chief Izuwa never forgave his daughter for marrying outside of their tribe. No family member had attended the church wedding. Not their father, certainly not his mother, nor his brother and sister. Afam had later called Ogugua to apologize and to explain that he had been in the middle of his exams at the time of the wedding. She had been gracious and thanked him for his trouble, but they both knew he was only making excuses. The family had not kept in touch with her after that. He did not even know when she gave birth to any of the children. It was as if she had never been a part of the family.

"What about your mother?" Binta Garuba's voice broke into his recollections. "Can she help? I know you have a brother and sister too. Can't any of you help your sister's children?"

"My mother?" His voice rose at the incredulity of the question. Take Ogugua's children to his mother? The idea was too scary to contemplate. This woman could not possibly know what she was suggesting. If those hapless kids went to live with his mother, she would likely starve them to death.

"No." He shook his head firmly. "My mother cannot help."

Binta did not argue with him. She did not seem surprised either, causing Afam to conclude that Ogugua must have confided in her new family the reason she had not kept in touch with her father and his family after her marriage.

"If I may be so bold, sir," Binta hesitated.

"Yes?" He noticed how her hands shook as she held fast to the handbag on her laps. "Since you can afford it, couldn't you hire a nanny to look after them? They are very good kids, believe me. They won't give you any trouble." Her lips had begun to tremble again. "Please."

Afam did not want that option either. To him, looking after children was a responsibility involving money and time and emotional commitment. He had the money, but he did not have any time or emotion to spare. And a nanny could only do so much. He shook his head again.

If Binta knew him, she would have recognized the tautness of his lips and the rhythmic shaking of his head as an expression of finality. His mind was made up. It was unfortunate, but there was no way he could take on the kids.

"I'm sorry," he frowned. "I can provide financial support for them. That's all I can do."

"What if you sent the boys to boarding school? You would only need to worry about them during the holidays," she pressed on. "And as soon as I am done my schooling, I will come back, and I will take them from you. I promise I will, sir."

He shook his head again. "And what would I do with the little girl? Send her to a boarding school, too?"

"No. Of course not, sir. She's only eight years old. But… but—"

"But nothing, Miss Garuba. I can't do it. I'm afraid I have to ask you all to leave now."

Binta locked eyes with him for a few seconds and finally nodded. Slowly, she rose to her feet, looking defeated. "Very well, then." She dabbed at the tears coursing down her cheeks again. "I thought that since Sister Ogugua had a family, there would be no need to take her children to an orphanage, but I was mistaken. She really had no family."

Bravely, she looked up and stretched out a shaking hand to him. "I thank you for your time, sir, but I am deeply disappointed."

Afam's heart was heavy and his conscience even heavier as he watched Ogugua's sister-in-law gather the stuff the children had left in the living room and stumble toward the door. Her lips were shaking as she fought the tears streaming down her face.

Hadn't he been the one complaining about his mother's maltreatment of his half sister all these years? Hadn't he been the one lamenting just now that he had not had the opportunity to do right by her before she died? Could it be that he was being granted that opportunity and that he was letting it walk away?

He heard Binta calling for the children and walked to the window. He watched as she motioned to the boys to pick up their backpacks and follow her. He saw the confusion in their eyes, heard the older boy ask why they were leaving, and saw the little girl eagerly reach for her aunt's hand. They turned to say good-bye to Amadi, and Amadi turned to where Afam stood by the window. His servant's gaze was filled with confusion.

Were the children hungry? He remembered their aunt say they had been on the road for two days. Was he sending them away homeless and hungry? Why hadn't she taken him up on his offer for financial help? Oh well, he could always send them a check. But how could he contact her after today? She had not left any contact information.

It was shades of Ogugua all over again. How many times had he seen this scene replayed where his half sister was concerned? Ogugua biting back her protests when his mother took her toys from her and gave them to Ebele; Ogugua rushing to do chores with the servants and waiting on her stepmother and half-siblings when she should have been doing her homework or playing with her friends; Ogugua staying home with the servants while the rest of the family traveled on vacations; Ogugua getting married without any member of her family at the wedding; Ogugua quietly accepting that her father had cut her from his will; Ogugua always being hurt by his family but never attempting to fight back, never complaining, never protesting, and never insisting on her rights. Was this the legacy his sister had passed to her children?

He was their uncle, after all, just like Binta was their aunt. He had a home they could live in, Binta did not. He had servants that could help look after them, Binta did not. He had a family, but Binta Garuba was an orphan. There were all kinds of possibilities with his circumstance, and almost none with hers.

Afam closed his eyes and massaged his forehead again. His family had taken everything away from Ogugua while she was alive. They had stolen from a little girl both her father's affection and her rightful inheritance. Was caring for her children now that she was dead too much for him to do? Was this his chance for atonement? Should he consult his family first? What if they said no? But he did not have any time to discuss the situation with anyone. The only time he had was now, and if he delayed one more minute, he could lose even that.

He could do it.

He took a deep breath, opened his eyes, and exhaled loudly. He would do it.

He lifted his eyes heavenward. *Ogugua, can you see me? I'm sorry, okay?*

He called from the window, "Wait!" as Musa began to shut the gate behind Binta Garuba and Ogugua's children. He ran his hand over the bridge of his nose and released another rush of air. His heart was aching, his shoulders sagging.

"Wait! I've changed my mind."

CHAPTER 2

A child belongs to everyone.

—African proverb

"How are they doing?" Afam asked when Amadi entered his study late that night.

"They are okay, sir, no problem."

"What is the sleeping arrangement?"

"The little girl wouldn't be separated from her brothers, sir. I had to bring in the mattress from the other guest room to make an extra bed on the floor. Peter is with her on the bed, and John is on the mattress."

"Which one is Peter?"

"The oldest one, sir, he's thirteen. John is twelve years old."

"I see."

"The young man sent his apologies for his sister's ceaseless crying and assured me that she'll be okay in the morning. She's been having a hard time with their parents' death, and now she's been forced to separate from her aunt and to live in a strange house with strange people in a strange city."

"That's true for all of them though."

"Quite right, sir, but the others are older. She's just a little girl."

"She's an albino," he pointed out, as though that explained everything.

"Correct, sir."

Afam looked helplessly at the man who had been his servant since he moved into this house more than four years ago. "Her skin is so pale it is almost transparent," he lamented. "Did you see the thickness of her eyeglasses? Her eyes were crossing and jerking without control. What am I going to do with her, Amadi? How did I get myself into this palaver?"

Amadi was older than his master and oftentimes played different roles in his service. This evening, he was the adviser and encourager.

"It may not be as bad as you think, sir. She's going through a lot of stress right now. Maybe that's why she can't control herself. Try not to worry about it, sir. My wife and I will take care of her."

"I don't mind the boys. They are normal." Afam did not appear to have heard him.

"So is the girl, sir. Albinos are normal people. They are just like everyone else. Their skin is pale, and their eyesight may not be so good. Apart from that, we are all the same."

"Do you know albinos can't go out in the sun? How will this girl cope in school? Did you see the thickness of those lenses? With her vision so bad, how can she even study? What if she goes blind?"

"I don't think you should worry about that for now, sir. She is already here. Let's take it one day at a time."

Afam sighed, got up from his chair, and closed the file he had been trying unsuccessfully to read. Amadi went to close the windows and draw the curtains. He turned to his master, frowning at the huge scowl on the younger man's face.

"If I may say so, sir, you did the right thing. They are your flesh and blood. You cannot turn your back on your family."

Afam made no response. He shut down his computer and switched off the table lamp. He shuffled his feet on the floor and reached for his slippers. Amadi switched off the air conditioner and picked up the empty bottles of water Afam had scattered all over the study.

"Did you see how terrified she was when her aunt told her she was leaving them with me? You would think I was a monster. All that screaming can't be good for her system. She may have damaged her lungs."

"That's children for you, sir. Our people say it is good for them to cry like this every now and then, that it helps to strengthen their lungs. I'm sure she'll be fine in a few days."

That could be so, but Afam had already made up his mind to get a doctor to examine her in the next few days, just to get the full scope of her medical condition. He needed to know what he was dealing with.

"What's her name again?"

"Kamdi, sir. Short for Otuakamdi."

Afam nodded.

"I placed the briefcase in your closet, sir. Would you like me to bring it out for you tomorrow so you can go through the documents?"

"What briefcase?"

"The one their aunt left for you, sir. She said it contains all their personal information."

Afam nodded. "Oh, that? Don't worry about it. I'll sort it out when I have time."

"Very well, then. Good night, sir?"

"Good night, Amadi."

As he prepared for bed that night, Afam wondered why Igbo people gave their children such predictable names. Ogugua, *comfort me*, was his father's name for a child who would comfort him after his wife's death. Otuakamdi, *this is how I am*, was a plea for acceptance by society.

His thoughts turned to the latest news about the activities of Boko Haram in northeastern Nigeria. Not satisfied with burning down churches and kidnapping boarding-school students, the terrorist sect was now targeting Muslims. Just recently, they had gunned down more than fifty people who were praying at a mosque because they suspected them to be vigilantes. As usual, the Nigerian police was missing in action, and the federal government appeared completely helpless.

If he had known that Ogugua had been living in Maiduguri all these years, Afam told himself, he would have tried to persuade her to come back south, as far away as possible from the reach of Boko Haram. She might not have taken his advice, but he would have tried. And maybe that would have countered the guilty feelings surging through his chest as he laid between the sheets and struggled to sleep.

*****

"Come on, Kamdi." Peter rocked his sister in his arms. "You'll make yourself sick if you continue to cry."

Kamdi sniffed. "I want..." *Hiccup...hiccup...*"I want to..." *Sniff...sniff...*"I want to be sick so..." *Hiccup...*"I want to be sick so I can die."

"No, you don't." Peter frowned at her.

She sniffed and hiccupped again, swiping the flowing tears with the back of her hand against her cheeks. "True...true to God!"

"Please don't say that, Kamdi. You know Mama won't be happy if she heard you swearing. Just try and sleep. Everything's going to be all right," Peter promised, trying desperately to believe his own words.

"I want..." *Hiccup.* "I want Mama," she sobbed.

Peter did not reply.

"I want Mama. I want Papa. I want Auntie Binta."

John came to sit with them. He took his sister's hand and squeezed it gently. "They're gone, Kamdi. Mama and Papa have gone to be with Jesus."

"I...I...want...I want to go too." She sneezed, followed with a quick succession of hiccups. "I want to go and be with Jesus too."

Peter continued to rock her. "Try and sleep, Kamdi. Close your eyes and take deep breaths."

John tried again. "Jesus is not ready for you yet, Kamdi. Remember what Auntie Binta said? Jesus is still preparing a home for us in heaven. When he's ready, he'll come and take us to be with him."

"But I don't want a home of my own... I'm too little..." She sniffed. "I want to stay with Mama and Papa. I want to stay in their home! I don't want a house of my own!" the little girl wailed.

Peter frowned at his brother, motioning for him to be quiet. "Remember what Mama used to say, Kamdi?"

The girl looked up at her oldest brother with a frown. *Hiccup. Hiccup. Sniff. Sniff.* "Wh-what did she say?"

"She said God has a plan for your life, a good plan just for Kamdi. If you die now, who is going to do for Jesus the work he wants you to do for him here? Who's going to tell your friends about his love?"

"I...I don't have any friends," she stammered.

"Well, you have me, you have John, and you have Auntie Binta."

"But you know Jesus already. You know him better than I do."

"Yes, we know Jesus. But maybe we will forget one day. Or maybe we'll deny him as Peter did in the Bible. If that happens, maybe God will use you to help us turn back to him."

"Oh."

"And you also have Uncle Izuwa," John reminded her, eager to contribute his piece. "Maybe he doesn't know about Jesus. Maybe you can tell him."

"Who is…who is…Uncle 'Zuwa?"

"You know, the person who owns this big house. He's Mama's brother, remember? He's going to look after us now that Auntie Binta has gone to school abroad."

The young girl's eyes welled up again, but she was getting calmer. And she was thinking hard.

"He doesn't like me."

"Who?"

"That…that uncle."

"Of course, he likes you. He wants to take care of all of us."

Kamdi closed her eyes and the boys watched her suck in a deep breath and exhale. "He doesn't like me," she repeated slowly.

Peter felt her slim body relaxing. The tremors were subsiding, and the hiccups were getting less frequent. He motioned to his brother again, and they both kept quiet so she could sleep.

He looked over to where John sat holding Kamdi's hands on the other side of the bed. He knew John was hurting too. His brother used to read the Bible every night, but John had not opened his Bible since their parents' death. Peter silently prayed that they would be fine. He was not sure what to expect from their new guardian, who had accepted them so grudgingly, but he was thankful all the same. Who could tell where else they might have ended up? Their uncle had been gracious. It was up to them to make sure he would not regret taking them in. Indeed, it was up to *him* to ensure that they would all be on their best behavior in this big house. Their parents would expect nothing less.

He looked around again. They were in a large room with a huge bed and an adjoining bathroom that connected to another bedroom. Each room was larger than anything they were used to, and he could understand why Kamdi had refused to sleep in the other room by herself. They wouldn't need that second bedroom, he decided. Kamdi would be too scared to be on her own. Besides, the three of them had always shared a bedroom. He would ask their guardian tomorrow if they could all stay in this room. That way, they would not be taking up too much space in the house.

Her even breathing told Peter that Kamdi was finally asleep. He shifted and tried to leave but stopped when she let out a quick succession of hiccups and held him tighter. He sat down again and continued to rock her.

"Don't leave me, Peter... Don't...die without me," she murmured.

Peter felt his eyes fill with moisture and took in a deep breath. He wished he could assure his little sister that he would always be there for her. If there was anything his young heart had learned from the turn their lives had taken in the last few weeks, it was that nothing in life is guaranteed. Not the protection of a father, not the love of a mother, not the comfort of relations, not today, not tomorrow, and not even the next breath. He heard his sister hiccup again and exhale loudly before her breathing stabilized. He was glad that he did not have to respond; the future was not his to promise.

Gently, he disentangled her arms from his neck, laid her down on the bed and took off her glasses. He covered her with the bedsheet.

"I think we should pray," John whispered to his brother. "I think we should ask God to help us so that Uncle Izuwa will not send us away. I'm scared. I wish I could cry like Kamdi, but that won't solve any problems. I know he doesn't want us here. Auntie Binta forced him to take us in."

Peter nodded. "I know that, but I'm glad he agreed, reluctantly or not. We have nowhere else to go. Maybe it was God that forced him to accept us, not Auntie Binta. Remember, we were already leaving when he called us back. Auntie Binta didn't have anything to do with that. It's up to us now to behave well, so he won't regret his decision."

John's throat tightened. "Let's also pray for Auntie Binta, so that God will give her a safe journey to Scotland and protect her when she gets there. And that she will not forget to come back and take us to live with her."

Each holding their sister's hand, the two boys knelt beside the bed. And they prayed.

CHAPTER 3

*A family is like a tree—it can
bend but it cannot break.*

—African proverb

The feeling of helplessness that had accompanied Afam to sleep on Saturday night still hung over his heart when he woke up on Sunday morning. He had always disputed critics who described him as too kind, too compromising, and too accommodating for his own good. Maybe they were right. He should have insisted on sending those kids away with their aunt yesterday.

What am I going to do with them? That question drubbed his mind as he went to his garage, threw his running shoes into the trunk of his car, and turned on the ignition. Which of their relations could he perhaps call to help with the children?

Slowly, he shifted the gear to reverse and guided the car out of the garage. When the ringing of his cellphone intruded his musings, he pressed hard on the brake and moved the lever once more to park. *Probably Okee*, he thought and opened the glove compartment for the phone. He was meeting his friend at Shell Club for a jog and an early morning swim. Maybe he was calling to reschedule.

"Hello?"

The person at the other end hesitated briefly before breaking into a torrent of hiccups. Afam scowled, a familiar irritation assailing his mind when the sound ended in a whimper.

"Vickie?"

"Yes, Afam." Her breath broke into another hiccup. "Yes... it's me."

Bright rays from the rising sun angled over his eyes. He reached for the sunglasses he kept in the glove compartment and stuck them on his nose while he waited to hear the reason for her phone call. The only sounds from her end were plaintive whimpers interspersed with hiccups.

"Are you okay, Vickie?" he finally asked.

"Yes, I'm fine. I'm just worried," she sniffed. "I have a bad feeling about your asking me to leave you alone for four weeks."

Afam looked out of the car and saw Musa waiting to open the gate. He signaled to him to wait. Leaning back, he adjusted his side mirrors and wound the air conditioner knob on the dashboard, all the while trying to compose a suitable response.

"It's not you, Vickie. I just need some space from everyone to sort out a few personal issues."

"That's just it!" she exclaimed tearfully. "I feel that it's me you are trying to sort out of your life. It's me. And I've been asking myself why. Why? Afam, why? What did I do to you? Please tell me so I can apologize. I don't like this at all. Four weeks is too long for you to be sorting out personal issues."

As her voice trailed off, Afam pictured her—late twenties, pouting painted lips, braided hair, and wide bright eyes set in a fair-complexioned face. He suspected that the tears he heard in her voice had been switched on to arouse his sympathy. Slightly irritated, Afam lifted his left hand to massage his forehead and, after a while, turned off the car engine and cleared his throat.

"I'm not trying to sort you out of my life, Vickie. There are too many things going on right now. I'm just trying to think things through. Besides, you know it hasn't been long since I came back from South Africa, so I have a lot of work to catch up on. It's nothing to do with you."

That was not exactly true. It had a lot to do with her, and they both knew it. He had no plans to marry her, and one of the things he was dealing with was how to get out of their relationship without hurting her feelings. She had announced to the world on Facebook that they were getting married, and he had only heard about it when his friends started calling to congratulate him. But he would not be manipulated into a marriage he never asked for.

Soon after her announcement, Vickie had quarreled with his brother and his mother. Afam was not overly fond of his mother, but there was something to be said about respect for elders, which Vickie hadn't shown toward the older woman. He had warned her that his mother was crude and rude, so she should have been better prepared to be polite when the two women met in his home. True to type, Phidelia Izuwa had immediately pounced on Vickie. *Where are you from? What does your father do? What is your educational background? What is your occupation? How many boyfriends have you had before my son? I don't believe you!* By this time, Vickie had had enough. *How many boyfriends did you have before you met your own husband?* she had countered.

With the two women at each other's throats already, Afam shuddered to think how they would get along if he married Vickie. A vision of a house on fire came to mind.

No, he didn't want to marry Vickie. And it wasn't because his mother didn't like her. *He* didn't like Vickie.

"I'm going to church today to pray for us," her sobbing voice jarred his thoughts. "God knows I didn't do anything to deserve this type of treatment. I know that your family has been feeding you lies about me. I am very sorry if I have offended anyone. You don't know how much I care for you, Afam. You're in my heart," she concluded on a quiet sob. "Always."

He made no reply, waiting for her to hang up before ending the call. For a few minutes afterward, he sat in his Land Rover wondering what Vickie would do if she found out that, thanks to her forwardness, his mother was now actively looking for a wife for him. Upon his return from Johannesburg four weeks ago, Amadi had given him a letter from his mother in which there was a photograph of a girl whom she said would make him a good wife.

Shaking his head in amusement, he turned the ignition again, shifted the gear to drive, and beckoned on his security man to open the gate.

*****

Peter Garuba woke up late that morning in a room already filled with bright sunshine. He checked the wristwatch under his pillow and realized that he had slept hard all night. It was almost nine thirty. His eyes swept the strange surrounding, and, as he remembered the events of the previous day, he looked over to the bed. But Kamdi was not on the bed. Startled, he sat up and rubbed his hands across his face. Almost immediately, he heard a toilet flush and his racing heart knew relief. His movement had disturbed his brother, and John stretched as he woke up, but he promptly closed his eyes again and pulled the bedsheet over his head.

Otuakamdi Garuba, her thick, long, golden hair, woven in curved ridges and furrows and held neatly on top of her head with a rubber band, her glasses hanging loosely on her nose, opened the bathroom door gently and met her brother's eyes across the room. Brother and sister stared at each other as Kamdi made her way to the mattress on the floor.

"You're awake," he said and shifted so she could sit beside him. He reached to push her glasses up her nose. "How are you feeling this morning?"

"I'm hungry," she said.

Peter smiled. "Do you know where we are?"

"Yes." She yawned. "It's that uncle's house. Auntie Binta brought us here yesterday." Peter sighed, relieved that she was fast on her way to recovery.

"You gave us quite a scare last night. We were all worried about you."

"Is he mad at me for crying? Will he send us away?"

"I don't think he will send us away today. But if you continue to cry like you cried yesterday, he may not have another choice. He doesn't have any children of his own, and he won't know what to do with you if you keep on crying."

"I'm sorry, Peter. I'll tell him I'm sorry."

Peter nodded and looked closely at her face. She had regained control of her emotions and was looking more like the beautiful sister he knew. Her albinism was not extreme, at least not to him. There were scattered freckles on her face and arms; otherwise, her skin was smooth and clear. Early morning tresses were peeping from the roots of the golden hair held tight in the slim cornrows. Her eyes were wide and light brown in color. But her vision was poor, and her eyes sometimes appeared not to work together. Whenever she was upset, like last night, they could jerk uncontrollably, something even he sometimes found disconcerting.

"Why do people have to die, Peter?" Kamdi suddenly asked him. "Why does Jesus take parents to heaven without asking them if they want to go and without asking their children?"

Despite his resolve to be strong, the oldest Garuba child still felt the heaviness descending upon his heart. "I don't know, Kamdi. I really don't know."

"I don't like it."

"Me too. But Jesus doesn't leave us alone when we don't have father or mother. He becomes our father and mother. And he uses other people to take care of us."

"Like this…man?"

"Yes. And you must address him as Uncle Izuwa. I don't want to hear you call him 'this man' or 'that man' again."

John, who had been listening quietly to the conversation, now stretched and yawned. "Don't you think it strange that Mama never told us about her brother or anything about her family for that matter? I don't even think he remembers that Mama was his sister. We were as much a shock to him as he was to us."

"Yes, I think that Mama and Papa didn't know him." Kamdi nodded. "It was Auntie Binta that knew him, and she brought us here because she needs someone to look after us when she goes to Scotland."

Peter leaned back against the bed frame as he stared at his siblings and countered. "Of course, they knew him. Mama didn't know she would die so soon, or she would have told us about him. He's Mama's half brother. Don't you remember how Auntie Binta explained it? Mama's mother died and her father married another woman who bore Uncle Izuwa and his brother and sister."

The little girl was quiet for a minute. When Peter looked up, he found her squinting at him. "Are you and John my half brothers?" she asked, folding her lips tight.

Peter looked bemused for a moment, and then his eyes cleared and widened. He reached out and cupped her cheeks, felt the tremble of her pursed lips. "No, Kamdi. We are your brothers, not your half brothers. Why are you asking such a question?"

Kamdi looked from one brother to the other before she shook her head and smiled brightly. "Nothing. I'm hungry."

They heard voices outside and looked at one another. They were not sure what was expected of them, but they decided to make themselves useful. Silently, they opened their suitcases and unpacked their few possessions. When Kamdi went to brush her teeth and wash her face, the boys changed from their pajamas and ventured out. They soon found the kitchen, and to their relief, Amadi and a plump woman were already taking food out to the large table in the dining room.

"Good morning, boys." The friendly servant smiled at them. "Are you all awake?"

"Yes, we are," the boys replied, eyeing the overfilled plates with unabashed hunger.

"Your sister is okay?"

"Yes, she is," Peter answered. "We wanted to come and see how we can help in the kitchen. What can we do?"

"How about you make sure that you all empty your stomach before breakfast? The wife and I have cooked enough here to feed three hungry horses."

"Three hungry horses. Oh, you mean us?" John's confused squint gave way to dimpled cheeks as understanding dawned.

"Of course," Amadi's wife replied. "I don't see any other hungry horse here, Amadi, do you? Which one are you, Peter or John? You can call me Auntie Nneka."

They liked Amadi's wife instantly. She was round-faced and plump, smiling brightly at them with genuine affection. Peter let out a sigh of relief. If this was the couple that would be looking after them while they lived in this house, they would be okay.

"Hurry and wash up and come back in fifteen minutes," Amadi directed.

"And don't let me hear any more talk about helping in the kitchen," Auntie Nneka wagged her finger at them. "I can't have boys running around in my kitchen. The only person who can help me is your sister."

"But she's little," John hastened to point out. "She's only eight years old."

"That's okay. She can still help me do things that eight-year-old girls can do in the kitchen."

"That means you boys can help me to clean and to look after the compound."

"We'll be glad to help in any way," Peter spoke for the two of them. "We can fetch water, we can wash clothes, we can cut the grass, we can—"

Amadi held up his right hand and interrupted him with a smile. "Good. I'm going to need help with all those, but not today. You boys go on now and get ready for breakfast."

Happy that they will be allowed to help with something, even if not in the kitchen, the two boys ran back to tell their sister the good news and to wash up. Kamdi's expression fell when she heard she would be required to help in the kitchen. Being the baby in the family, her mother had never required her to do anything more than her schoolwork. Their parents had believed that her sensitive skin would not survive the heat in the kitchen, so she had never done any serious kitchen chores. But their flat in Maiduguri was tiny compared to this large house with its humongous kitchen. Peter reasoned that she would be okay because the heat in this house was nothing compared to what they had experienced in Maiduguri and the balmy Port Harcourt weather was a huge contrast to the desert heat in Maiduguri.

"Just do your best," Peter pleaded with her. "If the work is too hard for you, John and I will help you."

Thus assured, Kamdi got ready, brushed her hair, and followed her brothers out to the dining room.

The table was filled with the type of food they had only eaten occasionally all their lives—cereals, scrambled eggs, pancakes, chocolate drinks, and fruit juices. Behind her eyeglasses, Kamdi's eyes rounded in wonder. When she looked up, Peter's eyes were on her, and he gestured for her to remain patient. There was still something he wanted to know. He cleared his throat.

"Excuse me, Uncle Amadi."

"Yes, Peter."

"What time should we get ready for church?"

The older man's eyes narrowed.

"You children want to go to church?"

"Yes," Peter answered. "Today is Sunday, sir."

"Of course, it is. I will have a word with your uncle and let you know. But I don't think you'll be going today. After your long journey from Maiduguri and all that happened yesterday, you should take today as a true day of rest. Unpack your bags, sleep some more, and start getting used to your new home."

There was a moment of silence as the children considered his words.

"Sometimes, we go for evening service," Peter offered. "If we're too late for the morning service, we can go in the evening."

"I'll speak to your uncle and see what he says. I'm afraid we are not churchgoing people in this house, Peter. Auntie Nneka here, she goes sometimes, so maybe she can take you when she goes, but not today. Today, you rest."

The children thanked him for the food as he exited the room. They blessed their meal and ate in silence. Somehow, they did not feel so hungry anymore.

*****

From his bedroom balcony, Afam could hear the murmur of young voices in the dining room downstairs. A strange sensation made its way down his spine and over the top of his arms. He exhaled, unable to concentrate on the newspaper he was reading. How on earth was he going to take care of three children? Not one, not two, but three! The whole thing was surreal, like a tale in a strange dream world. A bad dream world. He supposed he could send the boys to a boarding school as their aunt had suggested. But what about the little girl? Could he send her to his mother's when the boys would be away in boarding school? No, he shook his head for the hundredth time. Not if he could help it.

Thinking of his mother, Afam knew he had to tell her about the kids. He had reservations about doing that—he did not want to deal with the vituperation that would inevitably follow. But he also knew it was the right thing to do. He reached for his cell phone, dialed her number, and waited.

"Hello?" her low raspy voice streamed across the line.

"*Nne*, hello, it's me… Afam."

"Oh, Afam, you are back. Welcome home. Did you have a good trip?"

"Yes, I did. How are you?"

"We're all fine. Did Amadi tell you I came to your house while you were away in South Africa? Did he give you my letter?" Phidelia Izuwa was never one to beat about the bush.

"Yes, he did."

Silence ensued as each waited for the other to speak.

"Well?" she asked.

"Well, what?"

"Well, what do you think?

"About what?"

"Awele Martins, of course. Didn't you read my letter? Didn't you see her photograph?"

Afam sighed. He had ripped both letter and photograph into pieces and thrown them in the refuse can as soon as he had read them. Now he tried to remember what the girl looked like. "Yes, I saw the photograph…"

"So, what do you think?"

"I think she's…um…she's okay, I guess."

"Is that all you have to say? She is Chief Martins's daughter and she's beautiful."

"So?"

"Chief Martins was your father's friend and investment partner."

"And that is why I should marry his daughter?"

He heard the heavy grunt from across the phone and knew she was not pleased with his response. "I'm not saying you should marry her, Afam. What do you take me for? All I'm asking is that you at least meet her and see if she is not better than that crazy Vickie who has caused our family so much trouble from the moment she attached herself to you like a parasite."

He could concede on that one. Vickie was difficult to shake off. But so was his mother. Over the years, he had found that one of the best ways to calm his mother was to ignore her grumpiness and strike a normal conversational tone. He tried that now.

"I didn't know Chief Martins had a grown child. I thought all his children were still in elementary school."

"I knew the girl when she was much younger." Phidelia was agreeable to the new angle. "Awele was an only child for a long time. She was already a teenager before her two brothers and sister were born. Betty, that's her mother, had given up hope of having any more children when they came. Three children in three years, just like that."

Silence for a long moment as they both waited for the other to resume the conversation. Afam was not interested in Chief Martins's daughter.

"You say she's currently doing her youth service?"

"Yes, she's serving in the middle belt, teaching at a school in Ituandem. I have asked questions and have heard nothing but good reports about this girl. She's young, smart, and well-behaved. Betty told me many young men are already asking for her hand in marriage. I have already registered our interest."

Afam closed his eyes and forced his heart to remain calm. If he didn't think she would be angry, he would have laughed out loud. His mother would never change. She would never stop trying to control him.

"*Nne*, I've told you before, stop trying to run my life for me," his voice held a measured tone. "I don't like it! I will decide whether I'm interested in this girl, not you. As for my relationship with Vickie—"

"Forget that Vickie," she countered, totally ignoring his protest. "She is nothing but trouble. She wants to uproot and destroy what another woman has planted. She wants to reap where she has not sown. When your father and I were struggling to send you to school, where was she? When I was having sleepless nights with worry about your—"

Her words faded as Afam tuned her out. *Were all women like this?* he wondered. Vickie used her fake humility and coy ways to manipulate him. His mother commanded him around and if that failed, she would prey on his conscience. His sister, Ebele, mocked him all the time. The only woman who had never asked anything of him was Ogugua. Until now.

"*Nne*," he said quietly when there was a pause in her diatribe. "The reason I am calling is to tell you that Ogugua is dead."

"Ogugua? Who is Ogugua?"

"How about your stepdaughter, my half sister? Do you still remember her?"

"Of course, I remember her. Stop this foolishness, Afam. What do you mean Ogugua is dead? Who told you?"

"She's not only dead, *Nne*, her husband is dead also. They were killed in a fire that was set on their hotel in Maiduguri by Boko Haram terrorists. Now her children are living with me. Three children. I thought you should know."

For once, as far as Afam could remember, Phidelia Izuwa was shocked and speechless. Quietly, he pressed the red button on his phone, ending the call.

*****

At noon, Afam decided to check on his newest relatives. He hadn't heard any sound since breakfast—no TV sounds, no loud voices, just a murmur here and there. *It was either of two things*, he thought. They were either tiptoeing around the house for fear of disturbing him, or they had gone back to their rooms to continue their rest.

He came upon them in the backyard, the two boys bent over the tadpoles in the artificial water creek flowing through the garden while their sister watched them from her seat under the shade of the umbrella tree. Afam almost did not recognize the little girl. Cleaned up and rested, she did not look anything like the screaming brat he had met yesterday. She wore a light brown skirt and blouse, which accentuated her fair skin. Her light-brown hair was braided in cornrows that spiraled up to a bundle on her head. Apart from her overly thick eyeglasses, she looked completely normal. Okay, much fairer than the average fair child, he conceded, but she was not as bad as he had been imagining. And the sprinkle of brownish spots on her face was quite cute.

As soon as the children saw him, they froze and stared nervously at him. He did not know when the little girl ran to her brothers, but suddenly, she was hiding behind the oldest boy and peeping at him cautiously from his side.

"Good afternoon, sir," the two boys greeted in unison.

"How are you guys doing?" he asked, as casually as he could. "How are you all settling in?"

"We're fine, sir. We wanted to come and thank you for our food this morning, but Uncle Amadi said we were not to disturb you. We're sorry if we disturbed you, sir," the anxious words spilled from the oldest boy.

"No, not at all. You weren't disturbing me," Afam hastened to reassure them. "I just came down to be sure you are comfortable and have everything you need."

"We do, sir, thank you. Uncle Amadi and Auntie Nneka have been very kind."

An awkward silence ensued. They were waiting for him to speak, but he didn't know what else to ask them. Looking down, he noticed that the little girl had completely disappeared behind her brothers and could not help the ghost of a smile that flickered across his face.

"Your rooms are comfortable?"

"Yes, thank you, sir. But if you don't mind, sir, one room is enough for us. Kamdi cannot sleep in a room by herself."

"If that works for you, go for it." He shrugged.

"Thank you, sir."

He wanted to ask them about school but decided to wait until he got to know them better. It was already May, just two months before the end of the academic session. *How life changes*, he shook his head slightly. This time last week, he had no idea that he would be thinking about children and school calendars. He expelled a deep breath and tried to focus.

Conversation ended, he started for the door, but Peter's voice stopped him.

"Em...excuse me, sir?"

He turned to see the boy tugging at his sister from behind him, pushing her out to face him. "Kamdi has something to say to you, sir."

Afam turned fully to the terrified young girl. She was wringing her hands and shooting glances about her surroundings. Her eyes were rolling again. Afam felt sorry for her.

"I'm...I'm sorry, Uncle 'Zuwa."

Her words caught him by surprise. He had never been called "uncle" before. Certainly, not by a frightened child in a quivering voice who could not get the *I* before the *z* in his name. He smiled gently at her. "Why, what did you do?"

Kamdi shot a look at her brothers. John nodded his encouragement.

"I...cried."

"You did?" He did not immediately catch on to what she meant.

"Yes," her voice sounded smaller with every sentence. "Yesterday, I cried and cried and cried. Please don't send us away. We don't have anywhere else to go. I'm very sorry. I'll be a good girl, and I will help Auntie Nneka to cook in the kitchen."

Feeling for all the world as though the winds had been cut off from his sails, Afam stood speechless, staring at the brave little girl. He had not expected this. Not from her. Not even from her brothers. His heart filled with an unrecognizable emotion as he gazed down at their hopeful faces. A calmness settled over his heart. Maybe looking after Ogugua's children would not be as stressful as he was imagining. They seemed like good kids. Maybe he had done the right thing after all.

"Come here." He motioned to the little girl. She moved on shaky legs and stood in front of him. He stooped to her level.

"Look at me," he commanded, and she did, biting down her lower lip to stem their trembling. Were those fresh tears he saw glistening on her brown lashes?

"Now listen carefully. I'm not going to send you away, is that clear?"

She nodded slowly, dropping her eyes slightly, resting them on a spot close to his shoulders.

"Your mother was my sister. I'm sorry she's dead. I'm sorry I didn't come over to visit you when she was alive. But we're together now, and that's how it's going to be for a long time to come."

"How long?" the words were out before she could stop them.

"For as long as you need a home. Or until your auntie comes back to Nigeria and takes you to live with her. I will do my best to take care of you all. Does that work? Do you believe me?"

She nodded.

He glanced over at the boys. John was blinking away tears from his eyes. Peter looked on solemnly. Afam's heart squeezed in his chest, and he had a strange urge to hug someone.

"That's a promise."

CHAPTER 4

*A bird that flies off the earth and lands
on an anthill is still on the ground.*

—African proverb

Awele Martins took her mother's letter to her living room and, stretching fully on the sofa, she took out the single rose-colored sheet and smiled at the familiar cursive handwriting. Even though they spoke on the phone all the time, it was not unusual for her mother to write her letters. She sent greeting cards to commemorate every occasion—birthday, Mother's day, Valentine's day—every occasion that she felt was worth celebrating. Sometimes, she would write brief notes to tell Awele she was missed; but whenever she wanted to tell her something serious, like when her father underwent surgery to remove a suspicious kidney mass, she wrote a long letter to explain that there was no need for anyone to worry. *Putting my words down on paper helps me to think through what I want to say and to express my thoughts clearly,* she claimed. Awele thought it was old school, what with smartphones and emails. Still, she treasured every letter and every card. She liked it even more because although she spoke to her mom very regularly, the woman never let on that she had written a letter, preferring to surprise her instead. Like today. They had talked on the phone that afternoon, but she had not mentioned that there was a letter on the way. It had become a game between them.

Now she bent her head to the letter, but first closed her eyes to breathe in the faint rose fragrance her mother had sprayed on the sheet. The scent was still there despite almost two weeks of handling by the postal services. Not for the first time, Awele wondered how such a girly woman had birthed and raised a tomboy like her.

The last rays of the late afternoon sun were already advancing through her window blinds, turning her black curly hair to the color of indigo and giving her soft skin a light dusky hue. With wide-set eyes fringed with thick lashes, roundly curved cheeks, and a long neck, the outline of her face had the thoughtful concentration often found on a child. She did not believe it when people described her as beautiful. In her judgment, a girl had to be model-like slim to qualify. But her looks did not bother her. Neither was she particularly bothered by the spiritedness which was so much a part of her character. As she read her mother's letter now, some of this vitality burst out, and she broke into helpless laughter.

Oturugbeke! Her mother was matchmaking! Unbelievable.

They had talked about this as soon as she graduated from university, and the woman had agreed not to pressure Awele in any way about marriage. But here she was, starting off with a long-winded apology.

She had written:

> *Try not to be disappointed with me, my dear.*
> *After you introduced me to your doctor friend*
> *and he told me his intentions for you, I started*
> *to think it is time you met other young men, to*
> *consider the alternatives before you make your*
> *decision.*

I especially wanted to tell you about Afam Izuwa, whose father was your father's business partner until his untimely death six years ago. I haven't seen a lot of him since then, but if he's still what I remember, then I would like you to meet him and should he be interested, please consider him before you settle for your doctor friend. My recollections of Afam are that he is a quiet and gentle man, well-educated, and very smart.

Awele shook her head and suppressed her smile, knowing how awkward her mother would have felt as she wrote those words. She sat up and took a sip from the water bottle on her table before continuing.

Would you consider him if I told you that your father also thinks very highly of him? Phidelia (that's his mother) and I have discussed this extensively, and we both think that the two of you should meet as soon as possible. She couldn't find a more recent photo of him. This one was taken at his sister's graduation ceremony three years ago. (PS: I hope you won't mind, my dear, because I found two old photographs of yours in the house and I gave them to Phidelia to show her son.)

Awele's hand flew to her mouth, her eyes brimming with merriment. *Oh, Mother, you did not!*

She turned over the sheet.

I know you must be laughing your head off as you read this letter, Awele. You're probably calling your mother all sorts of names (meddling, old school). But humor me, my darling. Before you settle for your doctor, please, please consider Afam Izuwa. You know I want nothing but the best for my beautiful daughter.

It started as a giggle but Awele soon gave in to loud, uninhibited laughter. She couldn't help it. She laughed until she began to cough, and tears filled her eyes. Then she reached for her phone to dial her mother's number but thought better of it. *Two can play the same game.* She threw the phone back on the table. It was more fun to keep quiet about the letter, to let her mother stew over whether she had received it.

She looked at the photograph clipped to the letter and saw a young man in casual business attire smiling at a girl in a university academic gown. Broad-shouldered and tall, his features were well-defined, sculptured with planes and angles. There was the faintest hint of gold in his dark curly hair where the flash of the camera had caught it.

Not bad at all, Awele concluded. In normal circumstances, if she had met him by herself and he had shown interest, she would probably have considered him. Too bad he needed his mother to do the job for him.

As she reached for her laptop to finalize the instructions for the science fair she was organizing for the college, she gave in to another giggle. What would Dr. Ben say if he knew that it was his bold declaration to her mother that he would marry her after her Youth Service that had led her parent to begin this desperate search for an alternative son-in-law?

Awele shook her head again and laughed.

CHAPTER 5

*There is enough room for both the eagle
and the kite on the tree branch; may
the gods break the wings of the bird
that denies the other this right.*

—African proverb

Slowly, tentatively, the Garuba children began to accept and settle into their new life with their new guardian. After the confusion of the weeks following their parent's death, when every new day was fraught with new challenges, they were relieved to settle into a routine once more. The two boys would wake up every day at six thirty, first have a quiet time of prayers, then brush their teeth and shower before waking up their sister. While John went to help in the kitchen, Peter would wait for Kamdi to pray, brush her teeth, and shower. They would all meet for breakfast in the dining room, after which they would carry out whatever tasks Amadi assigned them for the day before retiring to their room. Kamdi was tempted several times to ask Amadi if she could watch the big TV in the sitting room, but Peter forbade her. He said the noise would disturb their uncle, and that the least they could do to repay him for taking them in was not to cause him any discomfort.

Amadi came home one day with a soccer ball, and, sometimes, when they knew their guardian was not home, the boys would set up goal post markers at the far end of the compound and challenge one another to a shoot-out competition. Kamdi never joined them because she could not stand the afternoon heat. While her brothers dribbled their ball, she would either go to their room to take a nap, to the kitchen to shell melons for Auntie Nneka, or stay on the porch to draw in her sketchbook. Of their guardian, they saw little of, something they didn't mind at all. They were still ill at ease with him despite his assurances that he would not send them away.

They missed their parents. Auntie Binta had called Uncle Izuwa the evening before her departure to Scotland, and Amadi had brought the portable phone to their room so that each of the children could bid her farewell. She had assured them she would be back for them before they knew it and made them promise to always be good.

Their uncle did not mention it, but they all knew they would be required to go back to school soon. Their preference was to wait as long as possible before stepping into something they felt would be yet another painful experience. Their parents had both been teachers in their old school. It would be awkward attending a new school without them.

They were at the breakfast table on Sunday when their uncle came downstairs. When he pulled out a chair to join them and asked Amadi to bring hot water for his coffee, a nervous silence fell on the group. If he noticed that Kamdi's eyes grew wider behind her eyeglasses, or that she shifted closer to John on the bench chair, Afam did not show it. Instead, he complimented her on her dress.

"You look very pretty today, Kamdi."

The little girl's head bobbed up and down, but she did not meet his eyes as she mumbled her thanks. John pushed her back as she began to crowd in on his space. Afam managed to keep a straight face.

"I like your bracelets, Kamdi. They are very colorful. Can I see?"

At this, she froze, and her breath quickened. After a few seconds, she held out her hand, and he gently touched the two bracelets on her wrist. They did look different.

"Very pretty. Are those seashells that I see between the beads?"

She shook her head. He noticed that her hand was beginning to shake.

"They're not?"

She shook her head again.

"What are they?"

Her response was to bite her lips and frown intensely at the table mat. Taking pity on her, Afam released her hand and turned to Peter.

"You're all dressed up this morning. Are you going somewhere?"

"Today is Sunday, sir," Peter reminded him. "We were hoping to go to church today."

"Ah! I see," Afam remembered Amadi saying something about the children wanting to go to church soon after they arrived a couple of weeks ago. He scooped a spoon of coffee into his mug and poured hot water on it. "Did you always go to church with your parents?"

"Every Sunday, sir."

"Your father was a teacher?"

"Yes, sir. So was our mother."

He picked up the mug and tried to let them down gently. "Well, I hate to disappoint you, but I don't go to church every Sunday. I go sometimes but not every week. I travel a lot, so it is not easy for me to belong to any church."

Peter nodded thoughtfully. "Amadi said we could go with Auntie Nneka. She goes sometimes too."

"I'm afraid you won't be able to go with her today," he answered slowly. "I need to check it out. I need to know what church she goes to, the time for the service, how far it is from the house, etcetera. There are too many bad things going on in Port Harcourt these days and I can't afford to take any chances with your safety. Do you understand what I mean?"

They did. And they suddenly felt ashamed of their presumptuousness. The compound was big enough to play and run about in, so they had never thought twice about Amadi's instruction that they not venture out to the street. Maybe this was why. It was for their protection.

"I'm sorry for not asking first, sir."

"That's okay. It's partly my fault. I should have explained these things to you when you arrived. It can be dangerous out on the streets, especially with your accent, and your being new in town. You will arouse curiosity, and it would be easy for bad people to single you out from the crowd." He reached for a slice of toast. "Give me time to see what I can work out for you guys, okay?"

The two boys exchanged a quiet look, and there was silence at the table for a few seconds.

"You don't need to make any special arrangements for us, sir," Peter said slowly. "We can have church on our own for now."

"You can?"

"Yes, sir. Our father often said that even two or three people can do church when they are together. And there are three of us, sir."

Afam looked at his oldest nephew with a mixture of amusement and admiration. He snapped his fingers. "You know, that's an excellent idea. Why don't you do that until we work out something?"

This seemed like a good idea, and the rest of the meal was spent answering his questions about their parents, their school, and friends. They had missed their second term exams because of the timing of their parents' death, so they would need to be tested for admission into the appropriate grades at a new school. Afam made a mental note to start contacting the private schools in Port Harcourt. There was a Montessori school not too far away from Rumuodalla Estate, which he had heard was particularly good.

Kamdi did not join in the conversation, concentrating instead on the omelet on her plate. But from the corner of his eyes, Afam could see she was listening to everything with keen interest. He wondered that even after more than two weeks, she was still tense around him.

After he left, John turned to his sister and hissed.

"You don't have to wear that bracelet everywhere you go. One day, you will be forced to tell everyone what it is, and they would think you are weird."

Kamdi looked at him defiantly. "I don't care. It's my bracelet, and it's my business. It's not anybody else's business."

"Let's clear up," Peter intervened, not wishing that his siblings get into a heated argument. They would only end up attracting unwanted attention to themselves. "Let's clean up and go to church in our room."

*****

Afam could hear them from his balcony. They were trying to keep their voices low, but he still heard them singing chorus after chorus, hymn after hymn. Some of the hymns were familiar—songs that he remembered singing on the few occasions he had attended church. Hymns like "My Jesus, I Love Thee" and "What a Friend We Have in Jesus." Those kids were something else. They seemed to follow a regular church routine—songs, prayers, and sermon. When they started the sermon, Afam expected to hear Peter speak, but it was John's voice he heard. He listened carefully to decipher what the boy was saying, but the sound was too faint.

His thoughts went back to his childhood. In the Izuwa family, church attendance had simply been a matter of routine. His parents, especially his mother, had attended the Anglican Church regularly, but he could not remember them reading the Bible together at home, or discussing the sermons they heard from the pulpit. The only time he remembered the family praying together was when his father fell sick. His mother had brought in a prayer group from some pentecostal church to pray for him. The team had fasted and prayed, but Chief Izuwa had still died. As he listened to these children's voices, Afam acknowledged that there was nothing his father or mother had told him about the church or about God that could have resulted in the type of devotion the Garuba kids were showing to their faith despite their unfortunate circumstances. He was impressed.

"Miss Vickie is at the gate to see you, sir."

"What?" he roared at Amadi. Afam felt the frustration not just in his voice but also in his heart. It was as if his private space was being invaded by strangers, and his no-good gateman seemed incapable of turning them away. At this rate, he might have to call off his vacation and just go back to work.

"Miss Vickie, sir," Amadi repeated. "Musa just called me. He's not sure if he should let her in since you said you don't want to see anyone."

Afam shook his head and bit down on his lips. Why wouldn't Vickie leave him alone? The farther he tried to get from her, the closer she seemed to run toward him. Maybe it was unfair to blame Musa, Afam conceded. Like most people, his gateman was convinced he was engaged to marry the woman.

"Let her in. I'll be down shortly."

Bowing, the servant left to do his master's bidding.

*****

Afam found Vickie straightening up from behind the staircase as he came downstairs. Oblivious to his approach, she was muttering under her breath as she dried her hands with a small towel. He wondered what she was frowning at with such concentration and cleared his throat loudly. The sound seemed to startle her, but she quickly donned a smile and met his gaze.

"Oh! Afam, you scared me." She hastily tucked the towel into her handbag and began to run her hands through her braids. She looked a bit rough, and Afam attributed this to the long journey from Lagos. But why were there blue specks on her hair? When he got to the last step, she hurled herself into his arms and hugged him tight.

"Please forgive the intrusion. I have missed you so much. I know you said you wanted to be alone, and, believe me, I tried to keep away. But I just couldn't bear one more week away from you."

"How are you, Vickie?" Afam sounded calmer than he felt. He tried to disentangle her arms from his neck, but she held on tight.

"Lonely. It's been too lonely without you. I missed you." He turned just in time for her advancing puckered lips to land on his right cheek. "Have you not missed me?"

Afam hesitated. He was not a cruel man, and he did not want to cause her grief. But perhaps now was as good a time as any to break the news to her.

"Vickie," he managed with a shrug, finally untangling her arm from around his neck. "I'm still on vacation for two more weeks."

"I know." She smiled, turning to sashay to the sofa. She sat down and crossed her legs. "But you know you're in my heart. I couldn't wait to see you. Asking me to keep away for four whole weeks is pure torture. Did you want to kill me?"

"Ah, Vickie." Afam shook his head and sat on the opposite couch. "You and I need to talk. Things can't continue like this."

"Shh!" She placed her index finger over her lips and looked at him languidly. Her wide eyes were beautiful, like pools of water. Something inside him was rising to the invitation he could see in them. "Not now, okay? Let's talk later. I am famished. I've been working a series of overtime for the past week to make enough money for my plane ticket. I couldn't ask you for it because I wanted to surprise you."

"I see," he grunted.

He had heard that one before and had no appetite for more of her surprises. Before her last surprise visit, his brother was still living in his house, his sister still respected him, and he still had a decent relationship with his mother. She had wasted no time in exchanging abusive words with his brother, who had told his sister, who had told their mother, who had come down to Port Harcourt, to see for herself the chit of a girl that was causing so much trouble between her children. And that was only the beginning. His family's relationship with Vickie could not have gone further south since that day.

Vickie gestured for him to sit by her, but he ignored her. He wondered if she knew about the traces of blue on her braids and if this was the latest fashion trend. If it was, he didn't like it.

"Where's your servant? Tell him to bring me water to wash my hands and a cold drink. I'm tired and dehydrated."

Afam did not like it when she referred to Amadi as a servant, especially in that condescending tone. "You just came out from the washroom. Why didn't you wash your hands there? And what's with all the blue color in your hair?"

"What blue color?" she hesitated. She spread her hands out and examined them briefly. "It's this stupid dye. I've been taking lessons in textile design, you know, working with tie-and-dye fabrics for the last three weeks. I had practicals last night, and now I can't seem to get the color off my hands. I must have spread it to my hair when I washed this morning."

Abruptly, she got up and headed toward the visitors' washroom. "I'll try washing them again. Please have your servant bring me a can of cold beer."

"Why are you learning tie-and-dye if the dye is going to mess up everywhere?" he called after her.

"Ah, it's because of you!" She laughed from the washroom. "Everything I do these days is because of you o! We're not even married, and you have already taken over my life."

She meant it to be a joke, but Afam was not smiling. He waited for her to come out of the bathroom before he picked up the conversation again, frowning.

"What do you mean that you're learning tie-and-dye because of me?"

"Of course, it's all because of you." She pouted, her eyes teasing. "A virtuous woman is supposed to be industrious, isn't she? After we get married, I don't want to be depending on you for everything. There's big money in fabrics now that the government has banned the importation of ready-made clothes from overseas."

Afam looked at her and shook his head. He gave a dismal laugh under his breath. "Vickie, there's not going to be any—"

"Relax. I was only teasing you," she interrupted him again, laughing loudly as she walked back to sit on the sofa.

Amadi brought a platter with beer and biscuits and stood by his master, waiting to pour the drinks, but Vickie waved him off.

"Go and continue with your work in the kitchen," she dismissed him. "Don't hang around here like a statue. It's creepy. We can pour beer into glasses by ourselves."

Amadi's passive eyes stayed on his master, waiting to be dismissed. Afam nodded to him. As soon as he left, Vickie stood up, poured the drink into a glass, and handed it to him.

"I can't have you watching me drink by myself."

"Thanks, Vickie, but I don't want a drink."

"You can't be serious." She came to sit by him, holding the drink to his lips. "Come on, Afam."

He turned farther away, but she laughed and kept bringing the glass to his face.

"Vickie, stop it!" He pushed her hand away and got up to stand by the window.

His dark frown finally got to her. She hissed on her way back to her seat with the drink.

"Okay, okay, Mr. Grumpy. Take it easy. Jeez, you still haven't changed. Always too serious. Allow yourself to have some fun, okay? Life is too short to waste it grumping."

She downed the drink and headed for the door. "I'm going to the guest room to rest and freshen up before lunch. We can talk later if you like."

This was exactly what she had done the last time she visited. His mistake then had been in allowing her to stay the night. By the end of that week, she was fighting with his brother and causing havoc in his life.

"You can't stay here, Vickie."

"Why ever not?"

"Because…because I'm traveling," he decided. "I'm going to the village. Today."

That stopped her short, as he knew it would. Vickie went still, all teasing gone. She turned toward him. "What did you say?"

"I'm going to visit my family in the village," he repeated slowly.

"So, I was right!" Her lips curled. "You have made up with your mother? That is why you decided to go into hiding for four weeks. They have succeeded in poisoning your mind against me."

Afam could tell she was angry from the way she spoke slowly through her teeth. He looked at her for what seemed like the longest moment, feeling insulted and disappointed. Her presumption that he would sever his relationship with his family because she had had a fight with them caused a bitter taste in his mouth.

"Believe it or not, Vickie. I am not in hiding. I am not hiding from anyone. And I have not discussed you with my family since the day you and my mom had your fight. Maybe you should come with me to the village and see for yourself."

She hissed, snapped her fingers, and beat her chest. "Me? Go with you to your mother's house? God forbid! Are you trying to kill me? You know she hates me."

"Well, you don't exactly like her either."

"But she started it. Or maybe it was Uwa who started it. He was the one who quarreled with me, and when I fought back, he ran to the village to get your mother. She did not even wait to hear my side of the story before she judged and started attacking me. Have you forgotten?"

Afam held up his hands. "I don't want to talk about this now, Vickie. I'm going to visit my family at Amakama, and you can come with me if you want. It's that simple."

"But I came to visit you," she protested. "I came from Lagos to Port Harcourt to be with you. You can't just leave me here on my own."

"On your own? Vickie, I'm not leaving you here at all."

She shook her head, one arm to her waist, favoring him with a long-suffering pose. "It would just be until you come back."

His eyebrows went up as he shook his head.

"Nope."

"Come on, Afam. I don't know you to be this mean."

"I didn't invite you here, Vickie. I specifically asked you to stay away until after next week but you chose not to honor my request."

She looked at him then, and he saw how quickly she replaced her anger with a smile. Only, the smile seemed forced; it certainly did not spread past her twitching red lips.

"Oh, the things women do for love," she teased. "I'll still wait for you, darling. I took two weeks off from work, so I have a lot of time. I can stay anywhere you want me to, but it will cost you o! Presidential Hotel is not cheap. Novotel and Imperial are quite expensive too."

Afam smiled again and shook his head. "I can call for a driver to take you to any hotel you want to go. But I know your sister lives in Port Harcourt. Why waste your money staying at a hotel when you can easily stay with Rachel?"

"My money? Afam, you won't pay for a couple of nights at a hotel for me?"

"Why would I do that when you have a practical option?"

"How about because I am your fiancé?"

"Vickie." Afam shook his head again. "You're not my fiancé."

"*Yet*," she finished for him. "We are not engaged yet. But we will be. You see, no other woman will ever love you the way

I love you. Not your mother, not your sister. Very soon you will realize that I'm your soul mate, the will of God for you, the life partner he chose for you before we were even born."

He just looked at her, unsmiling, determined not to rise to her bait. Besides, how could he respond to such malarkey?

Just then, they heard singing voices and she turned to him. "You are alone in this house, aren't you?"

Afam did not answer. He too was listening to the song from his guest room. It was a Sunday school song: "I have decided to follow Jesus, no turning back, no turning back."

"Afam, I'm talking to you. Whose voices are those? Who is singing in this house?"

Before he could reply, they heard a young boy's voice loudly declare, "In Jesus's name!" and the equally loud response from other young voices, "Amen!"

"What's happening here?"

Vickie was no longer the amorous woman trying to seduce him only seconds ago. Eyes narrowed, lips tightened, and breathing elevated, she looked furious. She started to walk toward the guest room, but Afam moved quickly and stood in her way. Taking her hand firmly in his, he led her back into the sitting room.

"Listen to me. The voices you are hearing from that room, the children in that room are my sister's children. They are living with me now, and I don't want you to go in there and disturb them."

"Your sister's children? Ebele has children?" she scoffed. "Since when?"

"No, they are not Ebele's children. They are my older sister's children. Their parents died recently, and they have been brought into my care. I don't want you to disturb them."

"Afam Izuwa, who do you think you're deceiving? Who are you telling lies to? You don't have an older sister. How come I have never heard of her?"

"Because you have never asked, and I have never told you about her." Afam's anger bristled at being called a liar. "You don't know everything about me, Vickie. We can talk about my sisters later, but you will not go into that room now and you will not disturb those children. Is that clear?"

She nodded with a look that said he had not heard the last of this. He watched her take a deep breath and try to switch on her smile again.

"Very well then, Afam. Have it your way. But I know this is just a test. You just want to see if my love can withstand this type of shock. It's okay. I get it. No problem."

Afam resisted the urge to laugh out loud. Vickie truly had a gift for crazy drama and for ascribing outlandish interpretations to innocent conversations.

Just then, her voice broke. Tears gathered in her eyes. As he watched them escape and roll down her cheeks to rest on her clenched lips, pity and irritation warred in his heart. He didn't want to hurt her feelings, but at the same time, she needed to know when to let go.

"Vickie, I didn't invite you here," he reminded her gently. "If you had given me a hint about your plan to visit, I would have told you not to waste money on a plane ticket."

"Now I'm beginning to understand why you were insisting on being left alone. You didn't want me to know about your visitors."

"They are not visitors, Vickie. They live here. This is their permanent home now."

"We will see about that," she bit out. She took a Kleenex and blew her nose. "Well, you'd better introduce me to these new relations. I need to know the skeletons in your cupboard before I walk down that aisle to you."

Afam turned away, suppressing his annoyance.

As if on cue, two boys came out of the guest room with a soccer ball and headed outside through the hallway. Afam and Vickie watched them run to the field.

"Why, they are just young boys, Afam. I can look after them for you while you are away. They can sleep in one guest room while I stay in the other."

"They are already in one of the guest rooms, along with their little sister. Thanks for the offer, but I am taking them with me to the village," he stretched the lie.

"There are three of them?" she yelled.

One of the boys set up the markers for the goal post and manned it as his brother began to give him his best shots.

"Yep, I have two nephews and one niece."

Vickie shook her head and smiled. "How cute, Afam. I'm sure you'll make a great guardian. Can you ask your servant to take my luggage to the spare room then? I just want to freshen up and rest for an hour or so before I take my leave. If you don't mind, that is."

*****

After Amadi dropped her luggage in the room and exited, Vickie took her time changing from her clothes, rearranging her hair, spraying on perfume, and preening before the dresser. She considered whether to go back to Afam for this big discussion he was after. She was no fool; she knew that he wanted to break up with her. What he did not know was that she was never going to let that happen.

Curiosity got the better of her when she heard the toilet in the adjoining room flush and a door open and close. Recalling that the two guest rooms shared the washroom, she opened her door gently, tiptoed across the convenience and peeped through the keyhole to see who was in the other room. She would talk to them and get to the bottom of this story Afam had suddenly concocted about relations she had never heard of before.

Instead of the boys, Vickie saw a little girl on the bed writing in a book.

And she froze.

Shaking, she slowly retraced her steps and fell trembling on the bed. Could that be?… No, it was impossible. But seriously, could that be Afam's…niece?

Vickie shook her head vigorously and pinched her cheeks hard to be sure she was not imagining things. Then she got up and walked across the washroom and peeped through the keyhole into the adjacent room again. The girl was still there, biting the butt of her pencil and frowning at the notebook she was trying to hold still with one hand on the bed.

Vickie felt a surge of heat wash through her. Somehow, she made it back to the room before a scream broke from her lips. She screamed again. And again. And again.

Afam and Amadi rushed to the room and found her doubled on the bed, with a clenched fist thrust in her mouth in a vain attempt to still the tremors coursing through her body. When she would not look at him, Afam caught her chin and urgently turned her to force eye contact. "What is the matter, Vickie? You look like you've seen a ghost."

Vickie shook her head and squeezed her eyes shut. "Oh my god! I…I…I mean…" She caught his shirt. "Afam, please tell me that…that girl in that room is no relation of yours. Please tell me she is not sleeping next door."

He firmly prised her hands open and took a step backward. "She is my sister's daughter."

"The albino?"

"Yes. She's one of us. She's staying in that room with her brothers."

Vickie grabbed his hand and looked earnestly into his eyes. "That is impossible, Afam. You cannot be related to an albino. Tell me it's not true. Please. Tell me that you... Look, you must get rid of her. She must leave at once."

"Get rid of her? Don't be ridiculous. What are you talking about?"

"You have to, Afam." She held him tighter, her teeth beginning to chatter. "This is serious. If you love your life, you must send her away. You cannot have anything to do with an albino."

Afam thought that for once he was getting genuine emotions from Vickie. She looked petrified. She could not stop trembling and she was not making any sense.

"Why, Vickie? Why do you want me to get rid of my niece?"

"Because she is trouble! Haven't you heard that albinos are bad luck? They are a curse to every family they come into. They cause accidents and sicknesses and barrenness in their families. Evil spirits follow in their wake. Theirs is the color of trouble. You cannot keep an albino under your roof if you are looking for progress in life. Don't do this to yourself, Afam. Don't do it to me. Please don't do it to us."

Now it was Afam's turn to be shocked. He had never heard such drivel before, and from the lips of the woman he was presumably going to marry. It was embarrassing to know that supposedly enlightened people in the twenty-first century would believe such nonsense, let alone parrot them, or be so affected by them.

"Besides, my family forbids albinos! My father must not even hear that I am considering marriage to someone with albino blood."

"Vickie, now you are sounding crazy. That is utter nonsense." He stepped back in disgust, firmly withdrawing from the fingers holding desperately onto his shirt.

"I am not talking nonsense," she insisted. "It's the truth. Albinos only bring trouble in their wake. If you don't believe me, ask Amadi here. He knows I am speaking the truth."

But Amadi only stared blankly at her.

She hissed, looking pointedly from one man to the other, then came to a decision. "You know what, you don't even have to ask me to leave. As long as there is an albino under your roof, I cannot sleep here. Not even for one night. I don't want their curse to affect me."

"I don't believe this." Afam shook his head in disgust. "Vickie, I thought you were a Christian. You spend so much time fasting and praying, yet you are afraid of a little girl who, by the way, is also a Christian, just like you."

"Oh my god!" Vickie ran agitated fingers down her braids. Afam noticed that his words had not even registered. "I can't stay here. Not with that girl in this house. I must leave. Now! Immediately! Amadi, call the driver. I want to go to my sister's house."

Afam looked at her, puzzled. "Are you sure you're okay? Should I get you something…water, maybe some aspirin?"

"No, I don't need anything. Yes, I'm fine. I must go. Now!" Vickie slung her handbag across her shoulder and picked up her travel bag. "And you know something else, Afam? I don't believe for one second that that girl is your sister's daughter. Somebody has put you up to this, somebody who knows my family. I will get to the bottom of this. You'll see."

As he watched her follow Amadi to the car, all Afam could think was that Vickie had really gone mad.

CHAPTER 6

Who knows how water entered
the stalk of the pumpkin?

—African proverb

The setting Sunday sun found Awele walking back to Magaji Estate from church. Once a month, she volunteered to teach Sunday school at Grace-Side Assembly. On those Sundays, she would attend the evening service and afterward, would walk the three and a half kilometers from the church to her residence. This was one of those Sundays.

Walking was her preferred exercise. It helped save on fuel, which was both scarce and expensive these days. And it afforded her more opportunities to experience this community she had been sent to for her National Service year.

Nestled within the middle belt of Nigeria, Ituandem was a rural community boasting modern facilities—a hospital, a market, an elementary, and a secondary school. These notwithstanding, most citizens of Ituandem lived in rural communes where the people fed on produce from their farms, their town crier struck his gong in the dead of night, and the rooster woke everyone at the crack of dawn. And Awele just loved it. There was a massive iroko tree at the end of the road, the turnoff into the village. The pathway was wide, bordered on every side by mango, udara, and palm trees, as well as by thatched houses, shrines, and sculptured tombstones. It would take two more turnings from there to arrive at the stretch of road that led to Magaji Estate, the gated compound where she lived.

As she walked home that Sunday evening, humming to the catchy tune of a song they had learned in church, she came upon a crowd of villagers, gathered in front of a thick bush. There were at least fifty people—men, women, and children—pointing, whispering, and muttering in their language. Ordinarily, Awele would have passed by, because she did not understand the language and did not want to get involved in any strange village ritual. But this evening, her curiosity got the better of her, and she found herself making her way toward the crowd, finding an opening between some women and stretching her neck to see what the fuss was about.

Almost immediately, she smelled and saw fresh blood on the grass, and followed the bloody trail into the bush with her eyes. Under a low hanging iroko tree was a makeshift shrine, constructed with sticks and leaves and palm fronds. Awele gasped. A dwarf table had been placed between the palm fronds on which sat the severed heads of three animals, all dripping fresh blood. The animals' tongues and teeth were sticking out, and there were gaping holes where their eyes would have been. A blood-stained white flag was placed right at the center of the table, surrounded with kola nuts and palm fruits. Smoke trailed into the evening sky from a clay pot filled with palm fruit residue right under the dead animals' skulls. The scene smelled of evil, and she felt her body recoil in response. She closed her eyes and put a hand on her chest to calm her quickening heartbeat.

When she would later recount the experience to her friends, Awele would wonder that she had only been at the scene for only a couple of minutes. It had all happened so fast. But she would clearly remember the horror and fear she had seen on the faces of the villagers at the scene.

As she turned away, she shook her head from side to side, trying to tune out the sounds and sights of the crowd, and to unsee what she had just seen. She continued her walk home on shaking legs, taking deep breaths, and pressing her hand down on her chest, willing her heart not to fear. The new song from church was quickly forgotten.

CHAPTER 7

The most beautiful fig may contain a worm.

—African proverb

"My turn, my turn!" Kamdi declared, looking excited as her brothers grinned at her. Without waiting for their response, she covered her eyes with her hands. "I'm counting to twenty, starting now…one, two—"

"No, wait. You're supposed to count down from twenty, not count up," John's voice stopped her.

"Okay. Okay. I know, I know. Go and hide. I'm counting down now. Twenty, nineteen, eighteen…"

Suppressing their laughter, the two boys tiptoed off in search of hiding places.

They played hide-and-seek on the main floor only, restricting themselves to their room, the guest room, the hallways, the library, the kitchen, and the dining room.

"Twelve, eleven, ten…"

Peter hid under the table in the library, hoping it will not be too difficult for her to find him. In the past, he would not have hesitated to hide in the most difficult places, but in this big house, he wanted to go easy on her so she would not be frightened. There was a large wall cupboard between the spiral staircase and the visitors' toilet. John fitted his slim body behind the cupboard and held his breath.

"Three, two, one…ready or not, here I come!" Kamdi giggled and opened her eyes.

Everywhere was still and quiet, and she listened very carefully for the slightest sound, watching intently for the boys to make the slightest movement.

"Ha! I know you're in the room, Peter. I'm coming for you…" She laughed and ran into their room. The boys heard her opening and shutting doors and closets and still managed to keep quiet. She soon came out of the bedroom and ran into the kitchen.

"Have you seen Peter and John?" She smiled hesitantly at the woman cutting *okazi* vegetables in the kitchen. Her confidence was growing with every new day.

"And would it be fair if I told you where they are?" Auntie Nneka asked her.

"No, but if I don't find them in three minutes, I'll lose the game," she responded quietly. "May I look in the pantry?"

"Go right ahead. I didn't see anyone go in there, although I think someone might be in the fridge."

"In the fridge?" The girl's large eyes wobbled with shock. "There can't be. It's too cold."

It took Kamdi a few seconds to realize that the woman was joking. She giggled and ran off again. The boys heard her opening the cupboards in the dining room and managed to stay still.

"John, Peter, where are you?" She called out.

Remembering to make it easy for her, Peter responded with a low chuckle, and soon she was pulling his hand from under the writing desk in the library, and the two of them were out in the hallway, searching for John.

"Hey, you have less than two minutes now." Peter glanced at the clock in the dining room. "Be quick."

"But I have searched everywhere," the little girl exclaimed plaintively. "I cannot find him. Do you think he's outside?"

"No, he's not," a deep voice replied. Startled, the children looked up and met their uncle's amused glance from the top of the staircase. The excitement died on Kamdi's face, and she froze in her tracks. But Afam, who was leaning across the banister, ignored her discomfort as he continued.

"I know where he's hiding, and it's not outside. You are really close to him now. Do you want me to show you?"

She shook her head and pressed a hand across her lips. Behind the thick glasses, her eyes seemed to grow rounder with suppressed excitement, and her voice fell into a whisper. "You can't say or I'll lose the game."

"Very well, but you've got to hurry. The clock is ticking."

"Is…is he in the…library?" she asked haltingly, managing a glance at her uncle. Peter laughed.

"Nope."

"In the kitchen?"

"Nope."

"Bathroom?"

"Mmm…" Afam winked at her. "Close."

Giggling, the girl ran toward the guest toilet and began to knock. "John, come out. We said no toilets, remember?"

No sound.

"John! I know you're in there. Come on out."

"Ten, nine, eight, seven…" She heard Peter counting down and looked up when her uncle's voice joined the chorus. "Four, three, two, one…"

The stopwatch chimed.

"Zero!"

"Not fair, John," she cried. "Come out now."

"But I wasn't in the toilet." John's laughter came from beside her. He stepped out from the cupboard by the staircase. "I was here all the time and you didn't see me!"

Peter and Afam joined them, laughing.

"What's that stuff on your trouser?" Kamdi wrinkled her nose at her brother.

"What?" He looked down. His brown pants were stained with a dull blue powder that looked like detergent. He hit his palms against the powder, and a huge mess spread across the floor. Horrified, Peter looked up at their uncle and quickly knelt to wipe off the stain with the hem of his shirt. Kamdi pressed her lips together and glanced fearfully around.

"What are you doing?" Afam sharply reproached Peter. "Come away from there, Amadi will clean it up."

As usual, the servant silently emerged with a broom and a dustpan. The children crowded to watch him anxiously despite their guardian's calling to them to leave well alone. Amadi pushed out the cupboard, disappeared behind it, and reemerged a few seconds later with the source of the stain—a small bottle had fallen from the top of the cupboard, with its cover unscrewed, and the contents had escaped. He had also found a white bird's feather and several tiny pieces of white fabric. He stared at the items for several seconds before sweeping them into the dustpan.

"What is that?" Afam asked.

"I don't know, sir, but I think Miss Vickie may have left it here."

Afam remembered that he had observed Vickie standing in front of the same cupboard when she had visited on Sunday. The same stain had messed up her hands and her hair. He saw the anxiety on the children's faces and hastened to reassure them.

"Don't worry about it. It's just dye," he said. "There's no harm done. Are you guys ready to play another round of hide-and-seek?"

The children looked up in surprise. "Will you play with us?" Kamdi asked, excitement creeping back into her voice.

"Do you want me to?" He smiled down at her.

"You can if you want to," she replied, "but you're very tall, and I don't think you can hide anywhere. Even I can find you easily."

Afam smiled. "Then I guess I can't play hide-and-seek with you. We have to find another game that I won't be too tall to play."

After they stopped laughing at this, Peter spoke up on behalf of his siblings. "I hope we were not disturbing you, sir. We didn't know you were home."

"No, Peter, you weren't disturbing me. But when you guys are done, I will like you all to meet me in the living room so we can discuss arrangements for your school. We need to decide where you'll go and when you'll start. I have some ideas I want to run by the three of you."

"Can we meet you in one hour?"

"Sure. That should work."

Afam's nod included all three children as he went upstairs again.

Hide-and-seek was not so fun anymore.

At Peter's signal, the siblings filed out to their room to tidy up. As they waited for John to change out of his stained clothes, Peter lay on the bed and clasped his hands behind his head. He closed his eyes, deep in thought. Images of their family getting ready for school together every morning struck a stabbing chord in his memory, and he let his mind wander. Their routine had been simple but effective. They would all wake up early and meet in the living room for family prayers. Then the boys would rush to the shared bathroom while their parents and Auntie Binta would head to the kitchen. After breakfast, they would all head out to the bus stop for the short trip to the school. Sometimes, they would all walk to school because it was not that far away.

Peter sighed. He desperately wanted to be strong for his brother and sister, but he missed his parents, and time had not yet taken away the pain. His father had been his best friend and confidant. There was no question too difficult, too personal, or too philosophical that he could not discuss with his father. The answers to some of his questions would sometimes result in discussions that lasted late into the night. The pain of their loss was sometimes unbearable, and he wondered if he could ever stop hurting.

"You don't have to cry, Peter."

He opened his eyes to look at his sister. A tear rolled down his cheek. He sniffed and sat up, brushed one hand against his eyes and nose, and drew her close with the other hand.

"Don't mind me. I'm just being silly," he muttered.

"No, you're not. I miss them too."

"I know you do, Kamdi. I know you do." His hug tightened. Brother and sister were quiet for a while.

"I think it was a good thing they were both teachers. That way, we got to spend a lot of time with them before, during, and after school. I feel sorry for the people who could have known them but didn't."

"You mean, like Uncle Izuwa?"

"Yes, like Uncle 'Zuwa," Kamdi's response was immediate, as though she had given the matter some thought. "He is a kind man, but he did not know his sister. He did not know she was kind and brave and very courageous. He did not know how she used to laugh and laugh until her eyes would fill with tears.

That's what I still remember so clearly. Mama's laughter. And he did not know our Pa. I feel sorry for him."

Peter lifted his head to peer closely at his sister. When did she become so grown up? He saw John hovering by the door and beckoned to him. The younger boy came and sat on the other side of their sister. When he reached out, she took his hand in hers.

"Kamdi is right," he confirmed. "I miss them all the time. I feel sad that we cannot talk about them with other people because they did not know them. Only three of us knew how much fun they were."

Kamdi's hand tightened in her brothers', and her face grew more pensive. "But I don't want to forget the good times we had by thinking only of the sadness in my heart that they are no longer with us. That's why I try to remember Mama's laughter. She made everyone so happy."

Peter nodded. He had not thought of it that way.

"I think you're right, Kamdi. Their memories will continue to live in our hearts and our thoughts, but we will try and be happy, both for ourselves and for them."

A heavy but comfortable silence followed Peter's words. The three children allowed themselves to bask in their memories of parents they would never see again this side of eternity. Peter fought for control, still feeling the weight of his responsibility as the leader of their small crew. He saw the sadness in his brother's face change to a grim determination, and he exhaled in relief. As for his sister, her face was tight with concentration, her eyes were shut, and she was muttering silently to herself. He did not wait for long before her eyes flew open and she asked, "Peter, John, do you think Ma and Pa have become angels in heaven? Do you think they are picking flowers in the garden of heaven for Jesus?"

CHAPTER 8

If you do not stand for something,
you will fall for something.

—Popular proverb

A familiar beeping sound sent Awele scrambling to retrieve her phone from under her pillow. It stopped before she could say hello. When she checked the caller ID, she saw it was Tokumbo, flashing her. This was what her friend did whenever she didn't have enough credit to make the call from her own phone.

Awele dialed the number and Tokumbo picked up immediately.

"Hi, Awele, how goes?"

"Nothing spoil. How your end?"

"I'm okay. Everything is fine."

Awele waited, knowing there was more.

"Guess what?" Tokumbo continued. "I heard from a very reliable source that it was your landlord that sacrificed those animals you saw under the *iroko* tree last Sunday."

"Really?"

"Yes. It is supposed to be a secret, at least that's what the lady who told me said. But I just had to tell you. I had to warn you so you would be careful."

It made sense, Awele thought. Over the last couple of weeks, she had noticed a stream of solemn-looking visitors flowing in and out of the compound. She had also observed several members of her landlord's family whispering at various corners of the estate and had been woken up several nights by the sound of midnight prayers in the compound. She had not given it much thought previously, but now, as she tried to digest Tokumbo's revelations, she was convinced that something was seriously wrong with someone in the estate. And she was sure she knew who it was.

"Maybe this has to do with Edem."

"Who's Edem?"

"You know, my landlord's son, his firstborn."

"You mean that young man that followed you to prayer meeting some months ago?"

"Yes, that's him. He has been sick for some time now. I didn't think it was serious, but it must be. Perhaps his parents have turned to juju for his healing."

"I thought you said the boy didn't live at home, that he had traveled to Cotonou for business."

"Not Cotonou. He went to East Africa. His mother said he had gone to work at a used car dealership. But things didn't turn out as expected, so he came home after a few months."

"So, what's wrong with him? Malaria? Typhoid?"

"I don't know, and his mother won't tell me. It's been almost two weeks now since I saw her and when I asked, she just said her enemies are after her son's life, and that I should be praying for him. I asked if they were taking him to the hospital, but she said no, that this was not a case doctors can treat. I even asked if I could ask Dr. Ben to come to check on him at home, but she said there was no need."

"That doesn't sound good." Tokumbo clicked her tongue.

Awele remembered the grotesque sacrifice she had witnessed last Sunday on her way from church and shuddered. "They must be consulting witch doctors," she concluded. "But I don't understand why they won't just take him to the hospital. Which parent will not take their sick child to the hospital when they fall ill? It's not like they cannot afford it."

Awele could almost visualize Tokumbo's shrug as she responded. "Well, it's none of your business. Please try not to get involved. Just mark your time there, maintain a low profile for the next eight weeks, and get out as soon as your youth service is done. Your landlord is a dangerous man."

"Edem must be very sick," Awele's voice was worried, her friend's advice not quite registering. She parted her window coverings and peered at her backyard. Her old Honda CRV stood right by her window. About a hundred yards farther, close to the back fence, she could see the Magaji family shrine. It was a mysterious-looking, windowless, small house built with sticks and mud, with thatched roof made from raffia palms. Its location was fenced around with alternate white and red fabric sheaths, and there was a big 'KEEP OFF' signboard at the entrance. She had never seen any action in that area—neither sacrifices nor witch doctors—but she knew that did not mean the family had given up on the traditional religion.

Awele had heard the rumors about Pa Edem from practically everyone who knew she lived in Magaji Estate. Over a decade ago, when Pa Edem had been the state commissioner of police, occult practices, armed robberies, and kidnappings had flourished. The criminals had been well-known in the state, and some arrests had occasionally been made. But most of them had been released after a few days in detention, and many of the policemen who arrested them had been dismissed from the force. It was believed then that many of the criminals either worked for the commissioner or were bound to him by some sacred oaths. As such, they had acted like they were above the law and had done as they pleased. But Awele didn't believe everything she'd been told.

"If Pa Edem is as bad as everyone is saying, why does he allow his wife to attend church? You know that she is a member of the Holy Saints Church in Ituandem. And I often see different prayer groups coming to pray in the house. More so in the past few weeks. I think she's been calling them to come and pray for her son's healing."

"Original cover-up, that's what it is. They just want to fool everybody so that no one can suspect them when they begin to terrorize the community with their rituals and occultic practices."

Awele was not convinced. "I don't know, Toks. All the rumors are based on events that occurred over a decade ago. I honestly don't know what to make of it all. After all these years he may have changed. People change, you know."

Before she received her deployment for the National Youth Service Corps program, Awele had prayed that she would be sent to a location where she could make an impact in the lives of those she was sent to serve. In the past ten months, she had served the students under her care with diligence, and she was hopeful that their diploma results will reflect all the hard work she had put in them. She had given it her best and already knew a sense of satisfaction that she couldn't have done more. Maybe she could also impact the Magaji family in whose house she was living. Perhaps she could convince them to get medical help for their son before it was too late.

"Awele, promise me that you will not get involved. You are only a youth corper. Your parents are waiting for you to come home in two months. Make sure you return to them with your head sitting squarely on your shoulders."

"Don't worry, Toks." Awele chuckled. "My head will be sitting squarely on my shoulders when I get home from youth service. It won't be sitting on your shoulders—squarely, roundly, or triangularly."

"Awele, I'm not joking!"

"Toks, relax. Lighten up," Awele protested, trying to be serious once more. She exhaled loudly. "I have Edem's cell number. He and I have corresponded several times since that day he came to fellowship with me."

"And?"

"So, I texted him. Last week. I said I'd heard he had been sick and that I was praying for him."

Tokumbo hissed her reproof.

"He replied to me," Awele continued.

"What did he say?"

"Just 'thanks.'"

"Nothing more? No information on the sickness?"

"No. But I was not surprised. He once told me that his father regularly checks his phone calls and text messages, so he is always careful what he writes."

CHAPTER 9

*Kindness is a language which the blind
can see and the deaf can hear.*

—African proverb

The house phone was ringing as Afam stepped into the living room. Thinking that Amadi would pick it up from the kitchen, he did not immediately react. Then, remembering that his servant had accompanied Nneka to the market, he dropped his water bottle and grabbed the handset.

"Hello," he said, wrapping his long fingers around the receiver and wiping a film of perspiration from his forehead with his free hand. The weather was so hot that even the air conditioner seemed to be blowing hot air.

He fully expected to hear Vickie's husky voice in response. Since the day she ran off from his house as though her pants were on fire, he hadn't heard from her, and although he was glad about it, he was a bit worried that he may have been too harsh with her.

"Afam, is that you?"

He groaned. A call from Ebele was a call from his mother. What did they want? "Oh, hello, Ebele. What a surprise! How are you?"

"I'm very well. Are you home?"

"Home?"

"In Rumuodalla."

"Of course." Afam frowned. Where else did she expect him to be? Then it hit him. "Are you in town?"

"Actually, yes. *Nne* and I are almost in Port Harcourt. We just drove past Obigbo Gate, and we're on our way to your house. I'm calling to be sure you're home."

Afam shook his head in exasperation. "You don't think you should have told me you were coming before you set off from Amakama? There's no food in the house, and Amadi has just left for the market."

"No worries. We're not visitors. We can take care of ourselves. Obigbo Market is on our way; we can always grab something from there if we need to."

"Okay then," Afam said. "Are you all sleeping over?"

"Yes, but only for a day or two, so you don't need to worry. We'll be gone before you know it."

"No, no, no," he hastened to reassure her. As if that was possible—Ebele was her mother's daughter through and through. "You are welcome to stay as long as you want. I just wish you'd told me you were coming. I could have been away from home."

"You know that's not a problem, either. If we get there and you're not home, we'll just turn around and go back home. It's only a two-hour drive."

"Okay, okay, Ebele. Just come. What of Uwadiegwu? Is he with you guys?"

"No, he's at school. It's just *Nne* and me."

"Good." He paused and took a deep breath. "I wish he was with you. It will be good to see you all again. It's been a long time since we have spent time together as a family."

"Oh," she hesitated, at loss for a retort, and he smiled because he had caught her off guard with his soft-spoken words. *Maybe,* he thought, *just maybe, if we had been kinder to one another when we were growing up like Ogugua's children are to one another, there may not have been so much tension in our relationships.* But Ebele lived in their mother's shadow and would soon become cranky like their parent if she wasn't careful.

Afam replaced the receiver and listened again, this time to the giggles floating to him from outside. Kamdi's laughter always made him smile. In a few seconds, John and Peter's voices joined their sister's, sprinkling the air with their infectious innocence. Intrigued, he strode to the window to see what his young charges were doing that was so fun. Peter and John had blindfolds on, and Kamdi was giggling and giving them directions on how to avoid walking into the obstacles she had placed between their location and the gate house.

Afam smiled again. In the past few days, the children were relaxing more and more in their new home. He was glad they had each other to play with and especially glad about the care and protectiveness of the boys toward their sister. They needed one another. They needed this time together—to heal and recover and cautiously step into the new realities of their lives.

When he called, they stopped their game. Motioning to his siblings to be quiet, Peter ran into the house to stand before him in the living room. The boy stood poised, ready for instructions, biting down on his lips.

"I'm sorry, sir. We didn't mean to disturb you."

"Stop apologizing," Afam admonished his nephew. "You weren't disturbing me at all. I called because something has come up. I would like to see all of you."

"I'll get John and Kamdi," Peter responded. He stepped out and promptly returned to stand before him again with one sibling on each side.

Afam stood looking at their military-like formation for a few seconds before he asked. "What do you guys know about your mother's family?"

The children looked at one another and shook their heads faintly. "Not…not much, I'm afraid," Peter answered.

Afam nodded. "I thought so. Well, you are about to meet my mother and my sister. They are in Port Harcourt and will be here very soon."

"Is your mother our grandmother?" John's voice broke the shocked silence that had greeted the announcement.

Afam drew a deep breath again, shook his head, and explained that his mother was not Ogugua's mother. He told them Ogugua's mother had died before their father married his mother. He spoke matter-of-factly, hoping to put them at ease, but as the conversation continued, he noticed the little girl withdrawing more and more into herself. Big brown eyes watched him behind the thick lenses, her lips trembled slightly, but she said nothing. He wished she would say something, and he felt his heart aching with sympathy for them. They had hardly gotten accustomed to the fact that they had been left in the charge of an uncle they'd never heard about all their lives, and now, with very short notice, they had to prepare to meet another set of relatives.

Peter gazed out of the window. Had Uncle Izuwa been their father, he would have plainly asked him whether his mother and siblings knew about them, how long the visitors would be staying, if they needed to move out of their room for his family, and if they should be worried. Instead, he kept silent until their guardian was done with his explanations.

"May we be excused, sir?"

Afam nodded. "You guys don't need to worry about anything, okay?"

They nodded and filed out as quietly as they had come in.

*****

The Garuba children did not want to worry about the expected visitors, but no matter how hard they tried they could not work up anything but the now-familiar feeling of insecurity. They sat on the edge of their bed and stared hard at the floor. Tears filled John's eyes, and he swiped the back of his hand across his cheeks. Feeling rather helpless, Peter squeezed his hand and patted his shoulder.

"All we need to do is to be on our best behavior, and we should be fine, John."

"I just wish that Ma and Pa didn't have to die. Or that one of them was spared for us. I'm afraid his mother will not like us. I heard Auntie Binta say she never liked our ma. Why would she like us if she never liked her?"

"But Uncle 'Zuwa said we will be with him forever," Kamdi's small voice offered hopefully. "Maybe we can pray and ask God to stop them from coming. Uncle 'Zuwa didn't sound excited that they are coming. Maybe he doesn't want them to come."

"No, we will not pray for such a thing," Peter remonstrated. "This is her son's house and she has every right to come here. If Ma was alive and wanted to come to your house, would you tell her not to come because John's or my children were in your house?"

Kamdi thought about this for a moment before quietly shaking her head.

"Remember Ma used to say that if God is with us, then we don't need to be afraid," Peter reminded his siblings. "That's all we need to pray for."

"I know." John shook his head again. "It's just not easy to keep trusting God when everything seems to be falling apart every day."

Peter squeezed his brother's shoulder and tried to smile.

"Let's not imagine the worst, John. Let's just take it one step at a time. Now, let's clean up before they get here."

CHAPTER 10

When the music changes, the dance changes.

—African proverb

This evening again, as with almost every evening these days, Awele had a feeling that something unusual was going on in Magaji Estate. It was only a quarter past seven, but the compound was eerily quiet. No TV noise from Ma Edem's bungalow, no children playing outside, and no music blaring from the boys' quarters. Awele walked to her window and peered outside, but even the servants were nowhere to be seen. On a normal day, by this time, she would hear their movements and voices as they debriefed on the day's activities. But there was no sound today. Something was not right.

She looked across at the ancestral shrine at the edge of the compound. It was a small mud house with thatched raffia palms for a roof. The door was made from matted sticks and palm fronds patched with mud. If there was a window, it would be facing the outer fence because she could not see it from her vantage point. Awele had once overheard Ma Edem berating her two young daughters for going to play too close to the shrine. It was their father's special place, she had told them, and nobody else—neither wife nor child nor relative—could go in there.

This evening, as usual, the shrine looked abandoned.

Awele continued to stand by her parted window blinds. Thinking and waiting. Waiting for a sign of what was happening in the compound.

It must have been at least ten minutes before the curtains of a far bungalow opened and she saw—first two, then three, and then more of the numerous young men that lived in the compound—gathering around an open window. They looked subdued and downcast; their gazes directed toward Edem's bungalow.

Then it hit her. Edem must have gotten worse. Or even... *no, it couldn't be!*

Sucking in a deep breath to still a suddenly racing heart, she clasped her hands together. "Oh God, please no!" she whispered. "Please don't let him die. Please help that boy."

The memory of the sacrificial animal heads under the iroko tree caused a quickening in her heart, and she bit her lips. What could be so wrong that they would readily assume it was beyond medical help and resort to traditional superstitions? Recently, several church prayer groups had been visiting the compound, most likely summoned to pray for Edem. How could one be an idol worshipper and a churchgoer at the same time? Prayers, juju, prayers, juju—anything except take the boy to the hospital for proper diagnosis and treatment.

Sitting on the bed made her feel helpless. Impatiently, she brought out her phone and scrolled down until she hit the message button. There it was—her brief communication with Edem almost three weeks ago. Did he still have his phone? Could she send him a message now without his father finding out? Was he even alert enough to read a text message? Or was he in a coma?

"So sorry to hear you've been ill, Edem," she began to type. "Please go to the hospital, the doctors can help."

She sighed again and bit her thumb. Should she send it? If his father ever read this, would he think she was meddling in his family affairs?

Then she heard muffled voices from the compound and ran to her window again. She carefully parted the curtains, peeped outside, and her jaws dropped in shock.

A tall, muscular man tying only a white sheath wrapper, his upper body covered with *nzu* white chalk tattoos, was backing out from Edem's front door. On his head was a cap knit with bird's feathers, and on his arms were multiple charms and amulets. Cowrie shells of different colors were tied to his ankles, and they rattled loudly as he took backward steps, the muscles of his bare back heaving and contracting spasmodically. He was holding a smoking clay pot, gesticulating with palm fronds, and chanting incantations loud enough for everyone in the compound to hear. Awele retreated to her room, making the sign of the cross over her face and chest. She had never seen a *dibia* witch doctor before, but she recognized this one instantly.

After only a brief hesitation, she ran to the window again.

A few yards from Edem's door, the *dibia* shrieked and threw cowries on the ground. He followed the path of the shells, drew something on the ground with *nzu*, and began to study it. There was another man with the *dibia,* chanting after him. The second man was also dressed in a black sheath cloth, his face was streaked with white paint, and he carried a black fabric bag across his shoulders. He was mimicking the *dibia's* movements and actions and beating on a small traditional drum.

Absolute silence fell on the compound; only the chanting of the *juju* priests could be heard. Awele saw from the triangular partings of curtains in the different houses in the estate that, like her, everyone was watching the unfolding scene from the safety of their bedrooms. *Were their hearts beating like hers?* she wondered. Or were they used to this sort of thing?

After studying the cowries on the ground for some tense minutes, the witch doctor got up and began to yell and dance in excitement, his minion doing the same. When he flung out his right hand, the latter reached into his black shoulder bag and handed the witch doctor a green bottle. The *dibia* poured liquid from the bottle on the ground and started his libations:

Gods of the sky, take this—
Gods of the earth, take this—
Mammywota! Owumiri, beautiful goddess of the sea, fine lady, take this—
Ojukwu, the fair, take this—
this is your portion.
Our ancestors, small and great, guardians of our land; guardians of this household, take this—
Drink! Drink to your hearts' content; Drink and speak to your servant.
Oh, our ancestors...

On trembling legs, Awele drew back from the window and fell on her knees. And began to pray.

CHAPTER 11

The lion does not turn around
when a small dog barks.

—African proverb

"Who is this and what is she doing here?" A heavyset woman was sitting on the sofa in Afam's living room and sneering at Kamdi, disgust evident in her twisted lips.

The little girl's eyes grew wide, and her lips trembled.

"Ot…Otua…kamdi, ma," she whispered.

"What?" the raspy voice sounded irritated. "Speak up so I can hear you."

Afam did not miss the frightened look that lit up the little girl's eyes or the way Peter squeezed the right hand that crept into his. The girl started to speak again, but fear froze her tongue, and her eyes started to roll helplessly. One tear fell on her cheeks, and she wiped them with her fingertips. Before Afam could intervene, he heard Peter's calm voice.

"Her name is Otuakamdi Garuba, madam, and she's eight years old."

"Is she Ogugua's child?"

"Yes, ma," the young man nodded, this time looking questioningly at his guardian. "Ogugua Garuba was our mother. My name is Peter Garuba. My brother is John Garuba."

"Hmm," the old woman hissed. "How come your sister is an albino? Was there an albino among your father's relations?"

Afam looked at her again, wondering whether she honestly expected an answer from the boy.

"I don't know, ma," the boy's voice faltered, then picked up. "God… God made Kamdi beautiful the way she is, ma."

"Shh," she lifted her pointer to her lips. "Don't give me that attitude, young man. I did not say she is ugly."

"I'm sorry—"

"*Nne*, that's enough," Afam cut in. "Leave them alone."

Phidelia turned to give him the benefit of a long-drawn and narrow-eyed stare. "Afam, why didn't you tell me about this? There are no albinos in your father's family. This child must have inherited this from her father, not from Ogugua. Such a pity!"

An awkward silence followed this announcement, broken only by Ebele asking everyone again to introduce themselves and studying them closely to decide which of them looked the most like her half sister. The little girl stood trembling between her brothers and refused to answer any more questions. John looked a trifle nervous, but Peter answered all the questions from his aunt and grandmother calmly, looking unaffected by the tension in the room. Afam was impressed but not surprised at his young ward's courage.

Ebele stooped before Kamdi and tried to talk to her, but the girl fixed her gaze at a spot behind the wall and bit her lips tight.

"That's an unusual bracelet." Ebele reached out and fingered it for a few seconds. Kamdi stood like a frightened statue. "Are those seashells?"

Gasping, the girl sucked in a quick breath and swiftly shook her head.

"They're not?"

Again, Kamdi shook her head vigorously.

"What are they?"

The girl's response was to turn to her brother with a silent plea for help.

"Okay, guys, you can leave now," Afam interjected again, firmly. Relieved, each boy grabbed their sister by the hand, and the three of them ran from the living room, seeking the shelter of their bedroom.

As soon as the door closed behind them, Afam turned to his mother. "*Nne,* you didn't have to do that. They are really good children, and there's nothing wrong with the girl. Albinism is not a disease."

"Stop your whining, Afam. You knew that as soon as I heard they were living with you, I would want to come and see them for myself. And now that I have seen them, I can tell you that I'm not happy with what I have seen."

Afam shrugged. What else was new? She was his mother, wasn't she? The same mother he had known all his life. "You didn't even see them before passing your judgment, *Nne.* Your mind was made up before you came here that they were up to no good."

"That girl will cause you much sorrow, my son. I don't understand why they brought them to you. Albinos bring bad luck to their families."

Of course, he knew about the society's stereotypes and prejudices against albinos. Why, only a week ago, Vickie had given him an earful, and a demonstration. But hearing those same words from his mother made him feel sad for the little girl who was making gentle inroads into his heart with every passing day.

"*Nne,* let's not discuss this now. Those children have been violently orphaned, and I expect you to treat them with sympathy and kindness as they try to get their lives back in order. Albino or not, they are my sister's children, and I cannot allow you or anyone else to chastise me for taking them in and providing a home for them." He shook his head. "Honestly, Mama, sometimes I don't understand you."

"It's the truth. Albinos are bad luck. That girl will cause you grief."

Afam shrugged again. "Are you now a prophet?"

Phidelia sent him a warning look before she continued. "Tell me, when was the last time you saw an albino?"

Afam began to say something and then paused, there was no way to get out of a conversation with his mother when she was determined to have her say.

"Exactly my point. Albinos are almost extinct from our society. And do you know why?"

Afam rolled his eyes and turned to Ebele, sighing when his sister shrugged and turned her attention back to their mother. He gave up the argument and followed her cue.

"Because they have all been killed off," she answered her own question.

A chilly silence followed her pronouncement. "There are many myths and superstitions about albinos in our society. Witch doctors have convinced everyone that albinos have magical powers, that their body parts can cure terrible diseases. They hunt them down like animals, kill them, decapitate them, and use them for juju."

Afam was quiet for a moment, and from where she sat across the room, Ebele was nodding in agreement. "I have to agree with *Nne* on this one," she addressed her brother. "Do you remember De Bekee, the albino in Amakama when we were growing up? He used to wake up very early to go to the stream to fetch water every day. You remember how he went out one morning and was caught by headhunters who killed him, dismembered his body and made away with his head and his internal organs? There's never been another albino in the village since then."

"That's probably because he was never married. He had no children, so no one got the genes," Afam reasoned.

"And, tell me, who would have married an albino?" his mother countered sharply. "Who wants trouble? Which family in their right mind will give their son or daughter to an albino in marriage?"

Afam lifted both hands and pleaded with his mother. "*Nne,* please I don't want to talk about this anymore. Your point has been made. Fortunately, or unfortunately, it is what it is. I have an albino child to take care of, and I am going to do my best to shield her from all these superstitions and prejudices. Please don't repeat any of these stories to the children. I don't want them to live in fear."

His mother shook her head firmly. "I don't agree with you. They should be told as soon as possible. How can they learn to be careful if no one warns them?"

It was always like this with his mother. She knew everything, she knew what to do about everything, and she found her way into every situation, especially the ones she was not invited into. He decided not to argue with her, hoping instead that whatever ill wind blew her to his house would hurry back to take her away.

"Ogugua has had the last laugh after all." They heard her mumble beneath her breath. "I always knew she would strike back."

"What are you talking about, *Nne*? You think this is retribution? You think she planned to have an albino child and then die and foist her on me? Why would she try to get back at me when you're the one that had issues with her? Why didn't she direct that the children would come to you upon her death instead of to me?"

"Stop your foolishness, Afam. I did not do anything to her. You can never prove that I maltreated her in any way. She's the one that turned away from the family. But if you want to apportion blame to anyone else for her estrangement from the family, then lay it at your father's feet. I had nothing to do with it. She was, after all, his daughter, not mine."

That's rich, Afam thought. *Blame it on a dead man.*

"Tell me what happened? How did she die? How did they find you? Why not her husband's relatives? Why you?"

Afam's hands went up again. "*Nne*, hold on. I don't have all the answers to that yet. All I know is what I was told. Boko Haram burned down their hotel in Maiduguri while they were at a school event. She and her husband died in the fire. That's all I know."

Phidelia looked at him as though he had grown horns. "And you believed it? Just like that?"

"What do you mean?"

"Are you sure you're not being conned? How do you know they are Ogugua's children? Your father told me Ogugua had only two children. Two boys. She never told him about a third child."

Afam shrugged. "Well, their aunt left some documents for me…a briefcase containing school reports, letters, and such things.

"Did you see their birth certificates?"

"Not yet, but I believe everything is in the briefcase."

Phidelia opened her eyes and mouth wide to stare at her son. "You *believe*? You're not sure?"

He saw the horror in his mother's face and a feeling of guilt rushed through him. She was right—he really should have looked more closely at those documents.

"*Nne*, calm down. Perhaps if I had known you were coming today, I would have studied the documents in detail so I can answer your questions. I interviewed their aunt thoroughly when she brought them, and I have spoken extensively to the children. They are Ogugua's kids all right. The boys resemble her a lot. It is possible the girl looks like her father, I don't know."

Phidelia's loud hiss could have summoned Amadi from the kitchen if he had been home, but he was not yet back from the market.

"Afam Izuwa, your father and I raised you better than this. Why do you like to take chances? You believe every sob story that every Tom, Dick, and Harry spins to you. How can you tell that these are Ogugua's children by merely interviewing their aunt, or just by looking at them? Where are the facts? Where are the documents? It is this your simple attitude that made that witch, Vickie, or whatever she calls herself, take advantage of you. And speaking of her, I hope that whatever relationship you had with her is over. I will not be alive and see you marry that girl."

"*Nne*, stop it." Ebele emerged from the kitchen bearing a tray laden with bottles of water and glasses. "Let it go. You have already told him how you feel about Vickie. She is his business, not yours. That's not why we came here."

"Yes," Afam spoke through clenched lips, breathing hard. "Why did you come? The last time you came, you told me you will never step foot in my house again."

"And you believed me?" His mother laughed mirthlessly. "Shame on you, Afam. You don't want your mother to come to your house? For your information, you are still my son. You did not bring yourself into this world—I gave birth to you. You have not become what you are today by only your efforts—your father and I sacrificed and invested time, labor, and money in your life. What is yours is mine. If I want to come to your house, I will...any day, any time. I will stay as long as I want.

And you will look after me like a son looks after his mother, whether you want to or not."

Exasperated, Afam turned to his sister for help.

"Why's she here? Why are you both here? It clearly wasn't because you were missing me."

His gaze locked with his sister's, but she merely shrugged and turned to their mother. "Ask her."

"Mama?"

"We're here for two reasons," his mother announced.

Afam closed his eyes and exhaled loudly, but his mother ignored him as she continued, tapping her feet angrily on the carpeted floor. Ebele poured a drink in a glass and came toward her but she waved her away.

"First, I need to know what you have to say about Professor Martins's daughter. Her youth service is coming to an end in two months. Her mother tells me there's a medical doctor who wants to marry her, but they don't like him. They would rather have you as their son-in-law than the doctor."

Afam shook his head. This was why she had come all the way from Amakama? He could think of different ways to respond to her unbelievable madness, but he decided he didn't want her trouble. "*Nne*, I don't even know her."

"But you have to try first and see what she has to say. You are a wealthy man. These days in Nigeria women are looking for rich young men. She will have to be very foolish not to consider your proposal. As I said, her mother is interested in this union and so am I. I want you to consider it seriously."

Afam let that go. There was no arguing with his mother whenever she wanted to pass her opinion across. He was feeling hot and thirsty, so he readily accepted the glass of water from his sister and gulped it down without a pause.

"All right, I've heard you."

"When are you going to contact her?

"Mama!"

"I'm serious. This girl is good for you. From what I have heard, there aren't too many girls like her these days. And if you ever in your head considered that illiterate Vickie for a wife, then you absolutely should marry this one, even without seeing her. The two girls are miles apart. Here," she unzipped her handbag and rummaged until she found what she was looking for, "I have her address and her phone number on this paper." She thrust a piece of paper at him, which he grimly took and shoved into his pocket. "I brought it again, just in case you have thrown away the one I sent you earlier."

"*Nne*, you said you came here for two reasons. What's the second reason?"

Phidelia made as if to continue on the same topic, but his stern look managed to stop her. She sighed and shook her head before continuing.

"The second reason we're here is because of Ogugua's children. As I said earlier, she should not have burdened you with them. I cannot allow it. I forbid it."

"You what?" Afam's sharp inhale held for a moment. Who did she think she was? "*Nne*, please!" He finally exhaled. "I'm okay with the children living with me. I'm not complaining, I don't need anybody's help."

"Don't argue with me, Afam. It's very annoying. Those children will be a burden to you when you want to marry. This is why I have come to take them with me to the village."

"You have come to what?"

CHAPTER 12

Help me discipline my child is not a
heartfelt request from a mother.

—African proverb

Awele was sleeping when she heard the commotion—hurried footsteps running up and down across the compound. *Armed robbers*, she thought, and her heartbeat quickened. The compound was fortified, wasn't it? Pa Edem was a retired police chief. How could armed robbers have come in? She lay still for a moment listening to the urgent, anxious voices. Her phone read 2:00 a.m. Then she heard a woman sobbing…a dog barking…a car engine cranking.

Heart beating, she shot up from the bed and ran to the window and carefully opened her blinds to peep. In the clear illumination of the moon, she saw Pa Edem and another man carrying someone into a minivan. Ma Edem followed closely, hands on her head, sobbing loudly. Awele watched her landlord get in the back of the vehicle, and the second man take to the wheels. When the security man opened the gate and the bus drove through, Ma Edem tried to follow, but he held her back firmly and shut the gate. Awele saw her landlady throw herself on the ground and give in to uncontrollable weeping.

Without thinking twice, Awele pulled her dress over her head, changed from her night gown, and ran outside. She met them in front of Ma Edem's bungalow. When she reached for the distraught woman, the security man let her go. Awele took the woman in her arms and hugged her tight.

"Is it Edem?" she asked, as she gently pushed the front door open.

"They have killed my son o!" She sobbed. "My enemies have succeeded at last!"

A cold shudder passed through Awele. "Is he dead?"

"Since my son came back from abroad with this terrible sickness, I have been begging God to heal him. What have I not done? What more can I do? Oh, I am done for! My life is over!"

Awele let her weep as she led her into her living room. Some of the house-helps and the children were up and were anxiously crowding around, everyone folding their hands across their heads or chests, gripped with the stark reality of human helplessness in the cold face of the grim reaper. There was not a dry eye in the room as she led Ma Edem to a sofa. Awele found a glass and filled it with water for the woman.

"Sister, wetin happen?" Awele recognized Ginika's voice as she burst into the room, and breathed a sigh of relief. At least, Ma Edem would have another adult in the house who could keep her company in her grief, and there could be no one better than her own sister.

"My son is dead," she spat out bitterly. "God has allowed them to take my son from me. After all my tears and my prayers, after all my fasting, after all my gifts to the church, after all his promises to heal every disease and protect us from our enemies, he has allowed my enemies to kill my son!"

"How, my sister? Please stop crying and tell us what happened. You told me the other day that he was getting better," Ginika asked again, but her words fell on deaf ears. With more tears streaming down her face, Ma Edem was beginning to tremble with shock. Awele abandoned the water on the table and began to wipe tears from the hysterical face with a face towel.

"My poor son! What did I do? What did I do to deserve this? God, why didn't you just strike me dead? Why didn't you take my life and let my son live? What did he do to you that you would take his life? Why didn't you answer my prayers? O God! O God! O God!"

The younger children started to cry. One of the house girls raised a lament. The others joined, their voices going louder and louder. Even the boys were sniffing and wiping away tears. Awele looked to Ginika to control them, but the woman was focused on her distressed sister. More people had gathered now, and the murmurs and sobbing had increased, making it difficult to follow Ma Edem's explanations.

"So, have they taken him to the mortuary? Is that where Pa Edem has gone?"

Ma Edem sucked in a deep breath and exhaled. More tears. She shook her head.

"He was still breathing when they left for General Hospital, but he will not last the night. He will be gone in the morning, mark my words."

At this, the cries went up again. A house girl threw herself on the ground and started rolling over. "Brother Edem o! Brother Edem o!" she lamented. All the house-helps, the children, and the young people added their voices, crying and calling for Brother Edem.

Awele's heart was beating wildly. She patted it and tuned out the commotion so she could focus on the woman's words. "You mean he's not actually dead?"

"Not yet. But he's as good as gone. His breathing was shallow and very fast. His body was very hot, and he was unconscious. He's not going to last the night."

Awele gasped. "Madam! How can you draw this type of conclusion? You made everyone think he is already dead!"

"He is. My enemies have succeeded. God has failed me o!"

"No, he hasn't!" Awele held her by the shoulders and tried to speak slowly for emphasis. "And Edem is not dead. Do you hear me, madam? He is not dead. Do not give up hope. God is not a wicked God. He is faithful. Just hold on, please. Don't—"

"Leave me alone!" Ma Edem pulled her hand away and stood up. Tears of bitterness streamed down her face. "You didn't see him. Lying there on the bed, struggling to breathe, sweat pouring down like rain, his body so hot. You weren't there. I was there. I saw him, and I know he's gone."

Awele closed her eyes in disbelief. The woman had buried her son before he was dead.

"As long as there is life, there is hope. Calm down, madam. Let us pray together."

"What?" the woman screamed angrily at her. "Did you say I should continue praying?… Praying again?"

"I…I…" Awele started, unprepared for the naked fury and scorn in the woman's face.

"Listen, Awele, I'm done with praying. I'm done with fasting, and I'm done with believing in God. Have you not seen how many prayer groups I have invited, night after night, to come and pray to him to heal my son? Do you know how much I have spent on those prayer warriors? They have come. They have prayed. And Edem is still dying. What else does God expect me to do, eh? Kill myself?"

Awele sighed, torn between pointing out that God is not a man who can be bribed with gifts and offerings, rushing to her flat to call Dr. Ben to ask for his help with Edem's admission and treatment in the hospital, and trying to calm down her landlady. She chose the latter and fell on her knees.

"Please, madam, let me pray. Let's not give up. Everyone"—she waved her hand—"gather round, let us all kneel down and pray to God for healing. Edem is not dead yet. God answers prayers. Let us ask him for divine intervention."

Still sobbing, the children and the house-helps began to kneel, lifting up their hands in supplication.

Awele led them in the Lord's Prayer: "Our Father, who art in heaven, hallowed be thy name, thy kingdom come, thy will be—"

"Awele, stop that rubbish and leave my house now!"

She looked up, startled at the hands dragging her up and the fierce anger in her landlady's eyes.

"Don't pray those useless prayers in this house. Go to your flat if this is all you can offer. I will not believe in a God that stands by and watches innocent children die. I should have listened to my husband when he wanted to take matters into his hands. My only son would have been alive now if I had listened to my husband."

Taking a deep breath, Awele got up slowly to her feet.

"Madam, the Bible says that God is not—"

"Don't tell me what God is and what he's not. He is not any of those things you want to say he is. He is not love, he is not faithful, and he is not good. If he is even one of those things, my son will not be dead now. Oh, my son! Edem, is this how it will end for you? My son…"

The crowd of family members started to wail again. Awele's heart twisted, and tears fell unchecked down her cheeks. She swallowed and shook her head. Biting down on her lips, she tried again, gently.

"But, madam, Edem is not dead. You just said he was breathing when they took him to the hospital."

But the woman only turned sorrowful eyes to her.

"Leave me alone, Awele. I just don't want to hear about God. He hurts those who trust in him."

Her words pierced through Awele's heart, the finality of her tone an outright slap on her spirit. "I'm sorry you feel this way," she managed quietly.

Ginika went to the door and opened it. "All right, Miss Youth Corper, your time is up. You can leave now. My sister doesn't want you here, and you're upsetting her more by arguing with her."

"I'm really sorry. I didn't mean to upset her. I—"

Ginika grabbed her elbow and firmly led her toward the door. "Just go."

A shiver ran through Awele, and she bit her lips to stem the surge of tears. She turned and found everyone's eyes on her. Swallowing the lump in her throat, Awele exited through the open door, her ears ringing with the mockery of the door that was firmly shut behind her and with the wailing voices that grew louder as she walked to her bungalow.

As soon as she entered her flat, she fell on her knees to cry. And to pray for Edem.

CHAPTER 13

*You can stop a bird from making a
nest on your head, but you cannot
stop it from flying over your head.*

—African proverb

"So, why don't you want your mother to take the children to the village?" Okee asked, as the two friends were escorted to their table at Riverside Restaurant. "It seems like the logical solution to me."

Afam shrugged off his cotton jacket and wrapped it around the dining chair. In a blue button-down shirt and jeans, he felt overly warm. He reached for the decanter on the table, poured cold water into his tumbler, and shot his friend a heavy scowl.

"The kids are staying with me. Period. It's not negotiable."

The restaurant was loud and crowded, so he had to raise his voice to be heard. Okee lifted a hand and motioned for him to lower his voice.

"All right!" His friend nodded, amused. "Take it easy. There's no need to shout."

Afam frowned into his glass before gulping the water down.

"It's just that since the children came to stay with you," Okee continued, "you have been second-guessing yourself, not sure that you can look after them by yourself. You do not have the time, you do not have the experience, and you do not have the desire to look after three children. Your mother has the time, the experience, and the willingness to take them off your hands and yet you refuse. I don't understand."

The two had been friends for just over two years, and Afam greatly appreciated their friendship. But it was clear that his friend did not know much about his family. If he did, he would know that shipping Ogugua's children off to his mother was not an option he would ever consider.

A murmur of voices caught his attention, and he looked across the restaurant. A young family—father, mother, and three little girls—sat four tables from them. It looked like it was someone's birthday. Afam counted eight balloons swirling from a heavy-looking metal tin beside one of the girls. Eight years old, same as Kamdi. His eyes narrowed in speculation. The birthday girl wore her hair in braids and had thick prescription glasses, also like Kamdi. One of her siblings said something, and everyone around the table laughed. He observed her shy smile, again like Kamdi. But the girl in the restaurant was as dark in complexion as Kamdi was fair. For that, she was luckier than Kamdi. She was not born with the color of trouble.

He turned back to Okee who was still waiting for an answer. "You don't know my mother. She doesn't want to look after those children."

He refilled his glass with the cold water and lifted it up to his lips again. "Okee, believe me, if those children go to live with her, even for one day, she will chew them into pieces and spit them into the garbage. Just like she did their mother. I cannot allow that."

Okee raised a dark eyebrow. "You're making her sound like a monster?"

Afam sighed and swallowed the remainder of his drink. There was a television on the wall opposite, and he let the images pass without a flicker of interest. "That is not far from the truth."

"How can you say that? She's your mother."

Afam chose his words carefully. "My mother was a woman scorned, and she has never forgiven her rival."

"What?"

Afam nodded as his frown deepened. "She and Ogugua's mother were friends and roommates at university. My father was engaged to marry my mother, but just before the wedding, he broke off the engagement. Three months later, he eloped with her friend and roommate a.k.a. Ogugua's mother."

Okee lifted his eyebrows. "You're serious?"

"Mm hmm. My mother never forgave her friend and blamed her for her broken heart, her broken engagement, and all the scandal the elopement caused."

Okee's eyes grew wider. "Is this a true story?"

Afam nodded. "Yes, it is. I used to wonder why she never liked Ogugua. Then when I was a teenager, my aunt, her sister, came to visit us. I overheard them fighting over how my mother was treating her stepdaughter. My aunt said it wasn't fair that she was punishing the girl for her mother's sins. I didn't understand what they were talking about, but when I asked, my aunt was very happy to tell me the story. Years later, I asked my father, and he confirmed that it was true."

"So, what happened? How did they get back together?"

Afam shrugged. "I don't know that part of the story. I just know that Ogugua's mother died at childbirth, and he married my mother three years later. For as long as I can remember, she always treated Ogugua like an outcast, and she made sure my father ignored her as well."

Okee raked a hand through his hair and leaned back into his chair. He wasn't sure what to say, so he folded his arms and rested them on the table.

"It makes sense, I guess. Your sister paid for the sins of her mother."

"And it should stop there. Ogugua suffered dearly for something that had nothing to do with her. This is why I am determined that as much as lies within my power, I will not let her children suffer the same fate."

"I see."

As the food was served, Afam's thoughts went over again to how much he did not mind having the children around. The bond between the three was easy to see, and the leadership the oldest boy provided for his siblings was amazing. They looked up to him, and he led them firmly and responsibly. Afam marvelled at the lengths all three children went to please him by staying out of his way. Apart from the occasional voices here and there, mostly when they were kicking their soccer ball around in his compound, no one would have guessed he had children in the house. And these days, instead of keeping away from them, he often found himself watching out for them. The boys were getting more relaxed with him, but the girl still ran off or hid behind her brothers every time she saw him.

Okee continued with the exit of the waiter. "I thought that letting your mother have the children would give you and Vickie an opportunity to progress your relationship to the next stage without any encumbrances. Family interferences can confuse relationships sometimes."

With a heavy heart Afam stared at his friend, aghast. *"Opportunity for me and Vickie to progress our relationship to the next stage...* What next stage? Really? Okee, are you serious?"

His friend shrugged. "Look, all I am saying is that if you are serious about Vickie you may need to make other arrangements for the children. Despite your good intentions, and despite the children's good behavior, they could cause complications for the two of you."

Afam pushed aside his food to glare at his friend, his brown eyes flashing in anger. This was the last thing he expected from Okee. How could he believe such nonsense after all he had shared with him about his relationship with Vickie? Wasn't his best friend supposed to believe and trust him? Wasn't he supposed to stand by him?

"Old boy, why you dey talk like this now?"

"Wetin you want make I say? If you don't like Vickie, then let her go. You keep insisting that there's no future for the two of you as a couple, yet every time I turn around, she's hanging around you. Let her go!"

"I've tried…"

"There you go. You're doing it again. What do you mean you've *tried*? You don't *try* with women like Vickie. Tell her to clear off and shut the door in her face if you are serious. That's the only way she will get the message. If you continue to pity her every time she cries, she will continue to bug you, and one day, she'll trap you into marrying her. Don't say I didn't warn you."

Laughter from the birthday family distracted him again, but he managed to pick up his fork and take his first bite of the salad before continuing.

"I'm never going to marry Vickie. I've told her expressly that it's not going to happen, that there is no marriage in our future, but she just laughs it off and continues as if she doesn't understand what I'm saying. She even paid me a surprise visit last week despite my direction that she stay away for a while. That's just how she is. She won't take no for an answer."

"You let her stay in your house?"

"No, I didn't. Nor did I have to."

"What happened?" Okee asked between mouthfuls.

"It was the weirdest thing. She got upset when she saw Kamdi and couldn't leave the house fast enough. She said she couldn't stay with an albino and that I must get rid of the little girl immediately. I haven't seen or heard from her since then, but I suspect she's staying with her sister at Shell Camp."

Okee waved his fork in his friend's direction. "This is another opportunity to tell her to get lost. What if the girl was your daughter, would she have asked you to get rid of her? Afam, you have to sit down with Vickie and tell her that it is over, and that you do not want her shadow to darken your doorsteps ever again."

Afam searched his friend's face and shook his head ruefully. "I'm...I'm not. I can't...Look, I will deal with Vickie in my own way."

But Okee was not done. "Honestly, Afam, what is the matter with you? Why can't you take a decision and follow it through? The Afam that I know is swifter and more decisive than what you are displaying on this issue. Are you sure that girl is not using remote control on you?"

Afam looked at his friend as though he had grown horns. "Remote control? You mean like *juju*? Okee, don't tell me you believe in that nonsense."

"What other explanation is there for the way she has you tied up in knots. She's in the driver's seat in this relationship. She's dictating the pace of everything, and you are just follow-ing her."

Afam shook his head. "Okee. Vickie is already history in my life."

His friend was not convinced. "I'll believe that when I see it."

CHAPTER 14

*Every river knows where its water
will not be soaked up into the earth,
and that is where it flows past.*

—African proverb

When Dr. Ben Adakole walked into the waiting room at Ituandem General Hospital, Awele stood up from the couch and met him just inside the door. "Did you see him?"

Never one to mince words, he immediately gave her his verdict on the situation, which was what she really wanted to know. "Yes, I did. That boy is very sick."

"But is he going to be all right? Do you think he will make it?"

The doctor turned sober eyes to her.

"It's hard to say. He presented with cerebral malaria, and by the time they brought him in, he was already convulsing. Right now, he is in a coma, and it is uncertain if and when he will recover."

Awele's heart sank. "But it is not just malaria, right? He's been sick since he came back from East Africa three months ago. If it was just malaria, it would have been cured by now, wouldn't it?" She sighed, shaking her head with confusion and impatience. "I'm still not sure why his parents didn't just bring him to the hospital in the first place."

The doctor looked grim. "I can understand that, Awele. You see, the malaria, if he can come out of the coma, could very well be the least of his problems."

"What else does he have, Ben?"

"I'm sorry, Awele. You should ask your landlady. I cannot go into details with you. You are not a family member."

"Ben, please! I know you know. What is it? Cancer, HIV? Why all the secrecy?"

"This is confidential stuff, Awele. Listen, I'm not even his doctor. I just went there to check out his admission notes for your sake. There are specialists working on his case, and I expect he will be here for a very long time. The malaria is not good, but it's only after that has been successfully controlled that they can start tackling the other things wrong with him."

Awele pulled in a deep breath and let it out slowly, trying to stay calm. She glanced at her watch; it was already after eleven o'clock. She had to pick up Tokumbo from school in exactly thirty minutes, drive her to the market, then to her apartment, and still get back to the school before one.

It seemed like a week since the confrontation with Ma Edem, but it was just two nights ago. She recalled the attempts she had made to speak with the lady yesterday to find out how her son was doing and the way she had been rebuffed. But none of that mattered in the light of Edem's sickness, and she had spent a lot of time since then praying for the young man. If he could walk out of that hospital bed healed and restored, perhaps his mother would believe in God again.

"At least, he's still alive." Dr. Ben touched her shoulder lightly. "Don't give up. I have seen my share of amazing recoveries in the years I have been practicing medicine. He could still make it."

She nodded.

"And again, he might not. Just don't go beating yourself up. Some things are beyond human control."

Again, she nodded.

"And please, Awele, you must thread carefully with this family. Your landlord has quite the reputation in this town, and I don't want you caught in any of his shenanigans."

Awele tried to smile. "Wow, Ben, thanks. You know, you and Tokumbo are on the same page on this one. But like I told her the other day, nobody in that family has given me any reason to be worried for my safety. I've been in that compound for almost a year now, and I have never had any issues with anyone. My landlady has been very friendly. So have the children, especially Edem."

"Hmm. Just be careful, okay?"

"I will."

"Good. Enough of all that now. What time should I pick you up for dinner?"

"How about you tell me where we are going and I can meet you there?"

"I'd rather pick you up. I don't think it is safe for you to be driving around town at night on your own. Especially in that old car of yours."

"I'll be fine, Ben. I've been driving for years."

"I think that is part of your problem."

"What?"

"You're too independent."

She laughed. "Tokumbo says that too. Are you sure the two of you are not exchanging notes about me?"

"Just be ready at six. I'll pick you up."

"Yes, sir!" She smiled and lifted two fingers to her forehead in mock salute.

*****

Awele did not see a No Parking sign anywhere, so she angled her Honda in the empty space between two other vehicles on the kerb. Beside her, Tokumbo scanned the roadside for any police or road traffic officers that might be patrolling the roads in search of motorists to harass into paying bogus fines and fees for breaches of nonexistent and fake parking laws.

"Keep the engine running," she advised Awele. "Let's wait a few minutes. You can't be too sure with *area boys*."

They waited, each wary of the semblance of peace in the roadside parking area. On week days, motorists and visitors to Ituandem Main Market could park along the roadside, but it was not uncommon to be challenged by street thugs, and since one could never be sure which road traffic enforcers were legitimate, everyone had to be on their guard at all times.

When no one approached them, Awele moved the car forward and killed the engine. Opposite their car, right across from a covered gutter, was a *Mama-put*, a roadside fish and plantain barbecue joint where a long queue of customers was waiting patiently to be served. The girls hadn't planned to buy any, but the savory aroma filled their nostrils, and Tokumbo wound down the passenger window.

"How much for whole fish?" she yelled to the vendor.

"Tell your friend make she no park there o! Make una commot for there! Road Safety dey come," the woman yelled back at her.

"What?"

"Them go tow una motor. Make una go park for another place!"

"What of all these people wey park here? Why them never tow their vehicle?"

"Make you go ask them yourself. Me, I no know. But no say I no warn you o! As for the fish, you go wait small. All these people when dey for line, na the same thing them want. My market na first come, first serve."

Tokumbo wound up her glass and turned uncertain eyes to Awele.

"Maybe I should drop you off and find a proper parking spot?" Awele suggested. "We'll reconnect later. I don't want to get in trouble with these thugs."

"Maybe you should," her friend agreed. "I can join the queue for the fish, and you can meet me here after you have parked."

No sooner had they agreed to this than two young men wielding long wooden clubs drove up on a motorcycle. "Hey, you! Wind down, wind down! Where your particulars?" they demanded.

In a heartbeat, Awele hit the power lock, reversed, and sped off with an ear-piercing screech. She drove for about three minutes before she saw a car pull out from a marked parking spot. She slid in the car to the open spot, paid the parking attendant, placed the receipt on the dashboard of the Honda, and the two girls stepped out and walked back to the market.

The afternoon sun was hot. Awele had anticipated this and was wearing a short skirt, a cotton blouse, and dark sunglasses. Tokumbo wore a long skirt and blouse made from the traditional *ankara* fabric—always a good choice for the hot weather.

Ituanden Main Market was divided into sections—foodstuff, livestock, provisions, building materials, bookshops, electronics, and more. As the girls made their way through the textile line and entered the furniture section, a woman with bales of colorful fabric materialized in their way.

"Fine sisters, make una come buy o! Nice lace from Hong Kong. I'll give you better price."

"Latest designs from Europe," another vendor shouted. "Designer shoes from Italy, assorted colors, with matching handbags. For psychedelic sisters like you. Come check them out. I go give you better price."

It took several minutes to find their way to the travel section. Tokumbo was shopping for luggage, and Awele had come along to help her friend transport the suitcase to her flat. The sweltering sun was intense, and by the time they reached their destination, both girls were sweating profusely.

The shopkeeper welcomed them warmly with glasses of ice-cold water and straw fans.

"Na waa for Naija!" Tokumbo exclaimed after gulping down the water and wiping off sweat with her handkerchief. "This heat fit kill person o!"

"My sister, wetin person for do na?" the shopkeeper commented. "This weather no dey fear person. Even air conditioner no fit cool down person body for this kind heat. E hot well well."

"Yes o! Na only God dey save person for this country."

"Na true talk be that! I beg, na wetin una find come? Na which box you want make I show you?"

"Make you wait small, madam. Make we siddon here first and cool down before we talk business."

"No problem, my sister. Make una siddon rest small. Take your time."

While they waited, Awele filled Tokumbo in on her latest encounter with her landlady. The story of the witch doctor elicited the most interest from her friend.

"Were you scared?"

"At first, I was. I've heard so much about them, but I've never actually seen a native doctor in action before. It was quite the experience, I tell you."

"Wow! Good for you. If it was me, I would have peed in my pants with fear, and for sure I would have left that compound that very night."

Awele laughed.

"Anyway, my sister, just two days after that incident, Edem's condition grew worse."

"Obviously the juju didn't work," Tokumbo concluded.

"That's correct. They finally realized they had to take him to the hospital. I went there this morning, and Dr. Ben said they should have brought him in a long time ago."

Tokumbo shrugged. "Nothing to do with you and me. It was their call. They are his parents."

"So? Being a parent doesn't give you the right to kill your child."

While they continued to argue and catch up, a young family—man, wife, and a little girl—came into the shop, enquiring after a large leather suitcase on the shelf. The girls watched the shopkeeper show them the suitcase, patiently explaining the features of each compartment.

"When your father travels abroad next time, he can conveniently put you in this luggage, and nobody will know you are traveling with him." She laughed with the girl as she unzipped the suitcase. "See how large it is!'

"Can I try it?" the girl asked. Awele estimated she was about seven years old. "Can I go into the *akpati* and we can see if it is big enough to hold me?"

Her mother tried to hush her, but the father said, "Of course, she can. Jump in, poppet, and let's see if you can fit in this box. Maybe there is a way I can take you with me wherever I go."

The shopkeeper helped the giggling girl into the suitcase. "See what I mean? There's even room for your dog if you want to travel with him."

"Zip it up!" the girl demanded. "I want you to zip it up. I want to see if Daddy can carry me in the luggage."

The woman looked at the father and shook her head.

"I don't think so. That's dangerous. Come out now. You've had enough fun."

"Please!"

"No."

"Why not?" The father laughed. "Let's zip her up, and I can carry her away."

The shopkeeper continued to shake her head, so the man reached over and zipped the suitcase shut. They could all hear the giggles from the girl in it, but at his wife's protest, he reached over again and unzipped it, and the girl jumped out.

"That was so fun, Daddy. I want you to buy this suitcase. We can even play hide and seek in it!"

Everyone laughed. Except the mother. She was not impressed. She took the girl's hand firmly in hers, and they moved away without making any purchase.

"That was creepy," Awele commented to her friend. "Imagine seeing your child swallowed up in a suitcase. That was probably why the mother didn't want it anymore."

The vendor shrugged. "Different strokes for different folks. They will come back, though. They can't find good suitcases like mine anywhere else in this market."

"Spoken like a confident saleswoman."

"I hear you, my sister. But na true I dey talk so. Una don ready to look?"

Tokumbo nodded and got up to follow the woman, but not until she sounded a final word of caution to her friend.

"About this Edem matter, Awele, please, please, please be careful. I can't warn you enough. That family is dangerous."

"Now you sound like Dr. Ben."

Tokumbo smiled. "You better listen to him then. He knows what he's talking about. We've both been in this city for a long time."

Awele shook her head and took another sip of the cold water.

"Speaking of Dr. Ben Adakole," Tokumbo continued. "What's the latest? Are you two getting engaged soon?"

Awele scoffed. "*Et tu, Brute*? You too?"

Her friend laughed. "Relax, you know I'm only teasing you."

"Well, I have told him 'no' many times, but he won't let go. Do you know that the last time my mother visited he told her that he is going to marry me after youth service?"

Tokumbo's laughter broke out in excitement. "Oh no, he did not! What did she say?"

"That he should convince me first and then convince my father before coming to her."

"Oh dear!"

"And you know what she did immediately after that?"

"No."

"She went home and started to look for a husband for me."

"You don't say!"

"And she found one too. She has now sent me the photograph and phone number of someone she wants me to consider."

Tokumbo's eyes were wide with incredulity, and she was torn between laughter and seriousness. "Are you serious?"

"Absolutely. When we get to my flat, I will show you the photograph. The guy is not bad-looking at all."

"Do they still arrange marriages in this day and age?"

Awele laughed. "I don't think she wanted to, but she panicked when she met Dr. Ben. She asked if I know that Dr. Ben is only nine years younger than my father."

Tokumbo was holding her sides with laughter.

"That's not fair, Awele. Dr Ben is not that old."

"Yes, he is. My parents know him. Mom was surprised to learn he's still single. I think they were all in university together. Mom totally panicked at the thought of my bringing him home as my fiancé."

Tokumbo stopped laughing only to shake her head and wag her fingers in front of Awele. "Seriously speaking, Awele, age shouldn't be a huge factor in marriage. Dr. Ben is a good Christian, a highly successful doctor, well-respected in this town, very handsome, and stinking rich. If you marry him, you will be financially set for life. Isn't that what we are all looking for in marriage, a rich Christian man to marry?"

"How about love? Don't you have to fall in love with the man you will marry?"

"Love *ke*!" Tokumbo scoffed. "My sister, I think that emotion is highly overrated! People fall in love just as quickly as they fall out of love. If you really consider it with an open mind, you could easily fall in love with Dr. Ben. What's not to love really? Unless you are considering the young man your mother wants you to marry. Is that it?"

It was Awele's turn to laugh in derision. "No way!"

"Then you should seriously consider Dr. Ben Adakole. Don't disregard him so flippantly. He's a good man."

Awele stopped to frown at her friend. "Maybe you should go for him since you like him so much."

"I wish I could. But he doesn't want me, it's you he wants."

"Well, sorry, he's not getting me. I have told him that several times. He just refuses to accept it. Maybe he wants me to say something that will make him angry so we can have a big quarrel and keep malice for the rest of our lives."

Tokumbo shook her head emphatically. "Impossible! Dr. Ben is not like that."

"I know," Awele nodded in agreement. "He's a good man. He has been a good friend and a great Christian brother. That's all he will ever be to me."

A thought suddenly occurred to Awele. "Toks, did you mean what you said just now, that you would have him if he asked you?"

"Of course I did. I really like Dr. Ben Adakole," her friend replied, not quite meeting her eyes. Then turning to the shop-keeper, Tokumbo changed the topic. "Madam, that suitcase you just showed that family…that's the one I want to buy, but not that one you put the girl in—I want a brand-new one. Na how much you go sell for me?"

CHAPTER 15

If one person says that you are a horse,
smile at them; if two people say that you
are a horse, give it some thought;
if three people say that you are a
horse, go out and buy a saddle.

—A Wild, Wild West proverb

"**I** have something to tell you," Phidelia Izuwa began as she joined Afam in the living room after supper one evening.

He turned from the TV. Something in her voice warned that he would not like what she was about to say. She had been in his home for over a week now. Ebele had gone back to Amakama, but his mother had stayed back, insisting she would only leave when she was good and ready. He had called off his vacation and gone back to work, partially hoping that the long days with only Amadi and Nneka to talk to would make her leave, but she didn't seem to be so inclined. She had friends in Port Harcourt, and he had even overheard her on the phone with one of them planning to go shopping together for her boutique at Amakama.

"I looked around your house today," she started. "I haven't done that for a while now. The house is too big, and I'm getting too old to just wander about aimlessly. But I thought it was high time I refreshed myself on the layout of the house. I wanted to know what you have done with all the rooms in the house, including the boys' quarters."

Afam turned back to the TV. It was either that or be rude to her, which would lead to another fight. It seemed that all they did these days was fight and exchange unfriendly words.

"You called it my house, ma. You do not live here. You don't need an inventory of every room in my house."

"Well, I was bored, and there was no one to talk to except those children," she continued, brushing off his protest, "and those ones have a habit of disappearing any time they see me, as if I were a masquerade."

Afam tried to follow the news on the TV.

"Anyway, when I toured your home today, I made two important discoveries," she paused. "Please turn off that television and listen carefully to what I have to say."

He pressed the mute button and turned to his mother. "Okay, Mama, I'm listening."

She rolled her eyes and shook her head. "The first thing I found out today is that you are being manipulated."

Afam gasped. Now he had heard everything. "Mama!"

"I'm very serious, Afam. Someone is using juju on you."

He reminded himself that he did not want a fight and swallowed his irritation. It was better to listen patiently than to argue with her. He clicked the power button on the remote.

She nodded. "Now, there is a bottle containing blue powder with white particles on the windowsill in the boy's quarters' bathroom. I thought it was for Nneka, but when I confronted her, she told me that it belongs to that witch that has been following you about since last year."

"You mean Vickie?"

"Who else?"

"Vickie is attending textile school in Lagos," he explained, "taking a class on how to make *adire*. She had that dye bottle the day she came to visit and forgot it here."

Phidelia Izuwa clicked her tongue and shook her head dismissively. "*Adire ke*? That's a lie. What she has in that bottle is a love potion, which she must have got from a witch doctor. When you mix the powder with liquid, it dissolves and the color disappears. She needs only to pour a small amount into your food or drink, and you will become like butter in her hands, ready to do anything she asks of you, like a *mumu*."

Afam shook his head in exasperation, closed his eyes, and blew out a deep breath. His mother's *wahala* was enough to drive a man insane. Why wouldn't she just go back to Amakama?

But again, he conceded, maybe there was something he was missing. Hadn't Okee implied something similar at dinner the other day—that maybe, Vickie was remote controlling him? Remote control, juju...same thing.

"*Nne*, how do you know this?"

"I was once young and foolish, you know. I have been involved in a fight over a man before, and I know what tools Nigerian women use. These potions have existed for as long as there have been witch doctors in this country."

Without thinking, Afam attacked his mother the only way he knew best. "Well, isn't it great that you and Vickie have some things in common after all—you both have experience with fighting over men."

Shocked, Phidelia stopped and stared at him.

"Was the fight over my father? Did you give him the potion before or after the death of Ogugua's mother?"

As soon as the words left his mouth, Afam knew he had gone too far. What was the matter with him? He did not even like Vickie, so why was he trying to defend her at the expense of his relationship with his mother?

"Talk to me like that again, Afam, and I will curse you," Phidelia's raspy voice was quivering with shock and anger. "I don't care how old you think you are," she bit out. "If you dare talk to me like that again, I will slap that juju out of your head."

Afam had the grace to look ashamed. His mother had no right to sit in judgment over Vickie, he thought. She was no better herself. But that did not give him the right to insult her. She was, after all, his mother. And no matter how much he wanted her to leave his house, he didn't want it to happen because of any act of disrespect from him.

"Contrary to what you have allowed yourself to believe over the years, Afam, you are my son and I love you. God forbid that I should see you in harm's way and turn my eyes away as if it is not my business. I am not telling you these things to win favors from you. I am only watching out for you."

"Mama, I'm very, very sorry," he said solemnly. And he meant it.

A heavy silence ensued as she fought to control her anger. Afam waited, a part of him still hoping that she would feel insulted enough to go back to Amakama. But Phidelia was not done.

"It is for your own good that I'm telling you this, Afam. If you like, take my advice. If you like, don't take it. That woman is controlling you with her love potion, and if you are wise, you will cut off every association with her. I had not even seen her juju before I told you she's a witch. Don't say I didn't warn you."

Nonsense, he thought. Why, in this day and age, am I surrounded by all these superstitious people—first Vickie, then Okee, and now my mother? These were all supposedly enlightened people. How could they believe in these things?

"The second thing I discovered today, Afam, is that there is something fishy about these children living in your house."

Afam felt his hackles rise again.

"I found the briefcase of documents Ogugua's sister-in-law left for you about the children, and I went through them carefully. There are school reports, baby photographs, family photographs, etcetera. There are newspaper clippings of the Boko Haram attack and obituary announcements for Ogugua and her husband." She was quiet for a moment, then Afam heard her mutter, "May their souls rest in peace!"

He stared at her for a few seconds, then joined her to bow his head for a moment of silence in respect of Ogugua and her husband. This was the first time Phidelia had expressed any sympathy for her stepdaughter's untimely demise, and Afam was surprised. Nevertheless, he berated himself for leaving that briefcase in the study and for not reviewing its contents before his mother got her hands on them. He waited now to hear what she had found in them that had led to her latest conspiracy theory. "You said there was something fishy about the children?"

"Yes. I only found two birth certificates, one for Peter and the other for John. I did not see a birth certificate for the albino girl."

"*Nne*, her name is Kamdi. And I'm sure there is some explanation. Maybe you didn't look carefully enough, maybe the birth certificate is lost, or maybe their aunt forgot to include it."

But Phidelia did not agree with his simplistic explanation. "I don't think she forgot. The documents were meticulously and carefully organized. My impression is that the files were opened years ago, and documents have been added over time. Maybe by Ogugua herself. The newspaper clippings could have been all that her sister-in-law added."

"Okay. I still don't get your point."

"The albino girl's file starts with photographs of her as a baby while her brothers' files start with photographs of Ogugua when she was pregnant with them, followed by their birth certificates, all well-arranged and dated. Now, if you look closely at her school reports, the albino was born August 22. In one of the files, there's a photograph of Ogugua speaking at a church event on August ninth of the same year."

"What are you trying to say?"

"In that picture, Ogugua didn't look pregnant."

Afam shrugged. There could be a thousand explanations for the seeming discrepancy, but they would all be lost on his mother. It could be as simple as a mix-up in dates, but he knew she was not that open-minded. Only her interpretation of an issue was the correct interpretation.

"I wanted to question Peter, the older boy, but I knew you would be angry if I interrogated him in your absence. In any case, he would have refused to talk to me. They are all terrified of me as it is."

For once, she had actually cared for his feelings and done something right.

"You must investigate this thoroughly and find out the truth. Call that girl that brought them to you. Ask her for the albino's birth certificate. I'm interested in what she has to say."

"Okay."

"And if she doesn't give you an acceptable answer, I suggest you get a private investigator. It should be easy enough to find out when and where Ogugua had that child."

"But for what purpose, *Nne*? It should be clear by now that there's nothing I can uncover that will make me send that girl away from her brothers. I promised them a home until their aunt returns for them, and I will keep that promise no matter what."

Phidelia looked at her son impatiently. "You're too simple, Afam. Hasn't it occurred to you that the child may not be your sister's daughter?"

CHAPTER 16

The dance of a millipede does not impress
the man who has seen the dance of a snake.

—African proverb

Awele crashed into her landlady—literally—when she stepped out of her apartment, just as Ma Edem hurried past her, her arms piled so high with washing that she had not seen Awele coming.

"I'm so sorry," Awele said, her wide eyes reflecting her shock and embarrassment. The two women hadn't met since the night Edem was rushed to the hospital. "I wasn't paying attention. I hope you aren't hurt."

"No. I'm fine. You *nko*?"

Awele bent to gather the few clothes scattered on the dusty ground.

"I'm fine." She handed her the clothes. There was an awkward moment as she watched Ma Edem dust the sand off the clothes.

"It's good I ran into you," Awele ventured. "I've been meaning to come over and see how you're doing. I just wasn't sure if I am still welcome into your home."

Ma Edem looked embarrassed. "I believe I owe you an apology. The other night, you were only trying to help and I treated you badly. I'm sorry."

Awele smiled, her eyes lighting up, her dimples deepening as she nodded. "I understand. Don't worry about it. Edem is getting better, isn't he?"

"He's not yet dead." Ma Edem's tone was sad and despondent.

"*Haba*, madam. You've started again."

"I'm serious. It's only a matter of time before my son leaves this world."

Ma Edem made to look away, but Awele's eyes caught and held hers. She could see that the woman was close to tears. "Please come into my parlor and I can help you fold these clothes," she offered.

Ten minutes later, Ma Edem was sitting on the sofa in Awele's tiny living room. Between sips of cold water, Ma Edem talked about how Edem had woken from the coma, how the malaria had been brought under control, but that the doctors were still keeping him in the hospital for more tests and observation.

"So, was it just the malaria or was there some other illness?" Awele asked.

The woman looked away. She seemed to struggle with finding an answer.

"You don't have to tell me if you don't want to."

"It's all right. It all started when he came back from East Africa. He started to complain about aches and pains all over his body, and he was tired all the time. An unusual tiredness. Like someone with no strength at all. The next thing we knew, he was having diarrhea and could not keep his food in his stomach. The food will enter through his mouth and before you know it, it's going out through the other channel. Then his stomach started to swell, bloating up like someone suffering from kwashiorkor. His father took him to see a *baba*, and he told us that Edem accidentally stepped on a powerful juju over there in East Africa. The juju was not meant for him but he stepped on it. The *baba* said it's that juju that is causing the sickness."

"Why didn't you take him to the hospital?"

"The *baba* said the cure is not in the hospital. He said the gods of that place he went to are angry with him for stepping on them and not making the required sacrifices for atonement. That is why they struck him with the incurable disease."

Given their recent past, Awele did not want to upset the woman again by calling her story ridiculous. But she had to find a way to make her understand.

"Even with that, madam, you and Pa Edem should have taken him to the hospital for a second opinion. Perhaps, if the doctors had seen him on time, they would have been able to help him. Some jujus cannot withstand the power of medical science, you know."

But Ma Edem shook her head.

"You don't understand, Awele. You don't know what you are talking about. You needed to have seen Edem to understand how serious his condition was. Still is. Everybody agrees that he is under a heavy demonic attack, straight from the pit of hell. Yes, he is in the hospital now, but the doctors say they don't know what to do with him."

Awele's heartbeat quickened, but she tried to keep the fear from her voice. There were too many cases where malaria symptoms ended up being symptoms of a much more terrible sickness.

"Did...did the doctors say what it is?"

Ma Edem shook her head sadly and whispered, "H-I-V! They say my son has AIDS."

"Oh no!"

Ma Edem shook her head again, and the simmering tears broke free. Even as shock waves rippled through her body, Awele's heart broke at the defeat and hopelessness she saw in the woman's face. She went to her, expecting to be pushed away, but Ma Edem let her hold her while the tears silently trailed down her cheeks.

"I'm so sorry." Awele's tears mingled with the woman's. "We have to pray for him. God can do anything."

"I don't know, Awele. I don't know…"

Ma Edem lifted her head from Awele's shoulders and looked straight into her eyes. "I meant what I said the other night, Awele. I'm done with praying. I'm tired of raising my hopes high and watching them dashed to pieces every time. I really thought that with all the prayers, with everyone calling on him, that God would hear from heaven and heal my son. But he didn't. Instead of getting better, my son's condition has gotten worse."

"God is not a man. His ways are higher than our ways. His thoughts are higher than ours. We cannot compel him to answer our prayers. All we have to do is pray and trust him. We have to trust that he knows what is best and that he will make it all turn out right."

Ma Edem sniffed. "I've tried, Awele. I've given him a long time to heal Edem. I was the one that convinced my husband that we should give God a chance. Pa Edem allowed me to invite different prayer bands to the house to pray for Edem. They even fasted, but God didn't answer anybody's prayer."

"But how can you say that? One week ago, you were crying because you thought Edem was as good as dead. But he's still alive today."

She paused to give the woman time to think about her words. Then continued, "I know it's not easy, but please, I beg you, don't give up. Let's pray that the Lord will show the doctors how to treat this sickness. There are medicines now, good ones that can help. HIV is no longer the death sentence that it used to be when it was first discovered. Some cases can be controlled."

Ma Edem continued to weep. She was sniffing and hiccupping, silent tears coursing down her cheeks. Then finally she said, "Awele, it's already too late for Edem. The doctors said his case is beyond them. So Pa Edem has decided to go ahead with his initial plan of consulting Chibala. He's traveling to Pankistum tomorrow."

"Who is Chibala? Is he an HIV specialist?"

For a few seconds, Ma Edem looked at her in disbelief. Then she shook her head.

"*Haba*, Awele! You don't know Chibala?"

Awele shook her head. "Never heard of him."

"Chibala is the most powerful medicine man in all of Nigeria. He makes the most powerful concoctions. They say he gets his medicines straight from the spirit world, and that if you follow his instructions, you will get exactly what you want. Everyone—politicians and businessmen—go to the high temple in Pankistum for consultations. I know one woman who said he cured her of cancer."

Awele shook her head. Another witch doctor.

"You're the one that has been insisting that we take Edem to the hospital. Well, he's in the hospital now, and the doctors can't help. So why shouldn't we try someone else?"

Awele bit her lips again, thinking of how best to convince the woman to stick to the medical doctors. Ma Edem continued.

"The way I see it, if it is true that the disease was caused by a juju in East Africa, then maybe it's only another juju, a more powerful juju, that can break the curse and heal my son."

Awele continued to stare at the woman, reluctant to say anything that would upset her more than she already was. Besides, what more could she add to what she had already said?

"If you want to pray for us, Awele, pray that Chibala does not ask for too much money. Some years ago, when my husband was sick, he went for consultation. By the time we were done with the prescribed sacrifices, we were practically penniless."

"What type of sacrifices?"

"They told us to find a female owl and cross her with a male eagle."

"Did you?"

"*For where?* Is such a thing even possible? That is why it cost so much money. We offered Chibala cash in lieu and he accepted. It cost us almost everything we had."

Awele sighed. "What can I say, Ma Edem. You guys are wasting your time and your money. Stick with the hospital. There are new medicines coming out every day. HIV can be controlled."

Ma Edem's response was to shift her weight on the sofa and turn her eyes to the television.

CHAPTER 17

A wise man uses his tongue to count his teeth.

—African proverb

Tuesday did not start well for Afam. Vickie was at his office very early wanting to see him. They had not talked since the day she had stormed out of his home because of his niece. He had tried calling her, but she wouldn't pick up his calls. But here she was this morning, just after 8.00 a.m, wearing a forgiving smile and waiting for him at the reception desk.

"Have you got a minute, Afam?" Vickie asked in her most humble voice, and he invited her into the office. He could not but notice the smirk she threw at his receptionist and how the latter rolled her eyes and shook her head. He turned to smile reassuringly at the woman before following Vickie into the room.

"I'm sorry I didn't return your calls these past couple of weeks," she started. "I'm afraid I wasn't feeling very well."

Afam saw her excuse for the lie it was. He still could not figure out why she had been so impacted by the presence of Kamdi in his house. In *his* house, not her house.

"I'm glad to see you're better now," he replied with the first thing that came to mind.

"Thank you." Vickie smiled. "The main reason I'm here today is because I heard your mother is in town. I would like to come and visit her."

Her request caught him off guard, and he stared at her like the proverbial deer in the headlights for all of ten seconds before he shook his head and said an emphatic "No!"

"Come on, Afam," she cajoled. "I just want to apologize and make my peace with her. I behaved badly the last time we met. I think this is the best opportunity I will ever get to make things right again, while she's in your home."

Afam shook his head again, firmly. He had enough trouble with only his mother in his house. Adding Vickie into the mix would be like adding a spark to an open gas well.

"Have it your own way, then," Vickie scowled. "But can I take you to supper tonight? At Riverside Restaurant. Just the two of us. It will be my treat." Vickie was smiling and batting her eyelashes at him. Her voice could have charmed the birds out of the trees.

"Unfortunately, I've made plans."

"Oh? Am I allowed to ask with whom?"

"I'm not going out, if that's what you mean. But I have to be home early today to attend to family matters."

It was not a lie this time. He had been trying to talk to Binta Garuba since the weekend. His mother would not let him rest until the issue of Kamdi's maternity was resolved. He had left two messages on her cell phone and would try again tonight.

"How about tomorrow?" he offered. "Are you free for dinner tomorrow? I can pick you up."

She beamed. "Of course. It's a date."

Afam doubted she would still be smiling after the date. He would take her out and he would tell her again, as firmly as he could, that their relationship was over.

CHAPTER 18

The frown on the face of the goat will not stop it from being taken to the slaughter.

—African proverb

The alarm on Awele's cell phone beeped, heralding the dawn of a new day. With great effort, she opened her eyes and blinked at the early sunlight that filtered through her dark green curtains. When she tried to get up, a sudden dizziness seized her, and she fell back against the pillows. Her breath felt hot against her cheeks, her head was pounding, and a strong chill was running through her body.

Malaria, she recognized with a sigh, recalling that the signs had been all over her in the past few days. With great effort, she reached over to the phone on her bedside table and switched off the alarm. Gingerly, she lifted aching legs to the carpet and tried to stand up, but blood seemed to drain from her head and a weakness swept over her, causing her to lie down again. She would try and rest for a few minutes before deciding whether to call in sick to work. *That would not be likely*, she thought, since she was coordinating final revisions for the senior students in preparation for their GCE diploma exams. It was important that she did not miss even one day of school.

Pains in her stomach woke her up two hours later. The chills had not let up, and her temperature was still high. She felt hot liquid stream its way down her throat and crystalize into a convulsive bout of nausea, which sent her rushing into the bathroom. Spent and weak, she returned and called in sick for the day. Closing her eyes again, Awele fell into a deep sleep.

Loud, persistent knocking on her front door woke her up. She looked at the time. Twelve thirty. Had she been sleeping all this while?

"Awele? Are you okay in there?" Dr. Ben Adakole's voice came through the door.

"No, I'm sick." She sniffed, as she let him into her sitting room. The shivers had reduced, and her temperature seemed to have come down, but she was still feeling cold. And weak. Throwing a wrapper around her shoulders, she laid back on her sofa and looked up at the doctor. "I think I have malaria."

"So I see," he replied, feeling her forehead with his hand and opening his doctor's bag. "When did this start?"

"Just this morning. I woke up and my head was pounding."

He nodded and used his thumb to pull down her eyelids to peer into her eyes. He checked her blood pressure and listened to her pulse. As he rummaged through his doctor's bag, she leaned her head back and studied him through half-open eyes. Dr. Ben was of medium build, dark-complexioned, and slightly plump. He wore his hair longer than most men, so that the tight kinky curls formed a short afro around his head. His long nose over bow-shaped lips on an oval face made him look distinguished, just like a doctor. The scattered spots of grey in his hair smacked of wisdom and maturity. Like most of the doctors she knew, he was always impeccably dressed, carrying himself with sophistication and dignity. Today, he wore a sky blue polo shirt on black jeans. She closed her eyes as another chill coursed through her body. *What's not to love* about Dr. Ben, Tokumbo had asked. He was a successful doctor and a committed Christian. She shook her head at the answer that sprang to her mind. *Nothing*. He was a good man. He just was not for her.

"What are you doing here? I thought doctors don't make house calls anymore."

"I'm off today, remember? I told you about it the other night."

She grimaced. "I'm sorry, I forgot."

"Tokumbo called me to say you'd called in sick for work," he explained, sticking a thermometer into her mouth. "There's a malaria parasite making the rounds now, and I suspect that's what you've got. Or it could be typhoid. Right now, I need you to go to the lab for blood tests. I have some painkillers for you. They will ease the aches and pains and give you the strength to get dressed before I take you to the hospital."

Awele swallowed the two tablets he held out to her, praying for respite from the pains in her joints and abdomen. She was generally in good health, but every few years, she would succumb to a malaria attack. The symptoms were always brutal, as if some force were eating her up from the inside, as if an invisible hand was pounding on her muscles, trying to suffocate the life out of her.

"What is that?"

She followed his gaze.

"What?"

"The suitcase. Are you already packing up for the end of your service year?"

She heard the anxiety in his voice and shook her head. It hurt when she moved. "It belongs to Tokumbo. I drove her to Ituandem Main Market to buy it," she explained. "We branched in here on our way from the market and the Honda broke down,—refused to start—so I couldn't take her home.

I'm keeping it until she can arrange alternative transportation. Or until I can drop it off for her."

The doctor clicked his tongue in reproof. "You and that car! That thing is junk and should be thrown away before it lands you in hospital with serious injuries."

Maybe that was what she did not like about him—his bossy overconfidence and his know-it-all attitude. He was right, of course, he usually was. But did he always have to sound so superior? Every independent vein in her body bristled when he spoke to her that way.

"Allow me to buy you a car, Awele. A brand new car that will be more reliable than that old Honda."

"Dr. Ben, please, not now. My head is aching. I don't have the strength to get into that argument."

"But you know I'm right. You need a new car. That contraption you have there is a walking accident."

She shut her eyes and managed a smile. There was no way she would consider marrying this man. She did not need anyone to control her life.

"I love my car. There's nothing wrong with it that a good mechanic cannot fix. If I need a new car, I will ask my father, and he will buy one for me."

He was not happy with her answer. Awele watched the downturn of his lips and smiled inwardly at the cuteness of his sulk.

"Okay, I get it. You don't want me to buy you a car. But I bet that your father doesn't know the state of this car, or he would have done something about it already. Just give me the keys and I'll arrange for my mechanic to take it to the garage."

Awele extracted the single key from her bunch and gratefully passed it to him. "Thanks. They say sometimes a girl needs to stop arguing."

Ten minutes later, she locked up her flat and followed him out. His driver was waiting in the black Mercedes and ran to open the back door for her. As he joined her in the back seat, Dr. Ben commented on how quiet the compound was. "Where are all the people I see milling around every time I come here?"

"Ma Edem would have gone to the hospital to visit Edem," she explained. "The little children should be in school by now, and the young men will be at the market."

The gateman swung the gate open and stood on one side for them to exit. Awele wound down the window and explained to him that she was ill and going to the hospital. "Please help me tell madam," she pleaded through trembling lips, "in case I don't come back today."

"Speaking of your friend, Edem," Dr. Ben began. He wound down his window as they drove out of the estate and a cool breeze swept over the hot perspiration rushing down her face. She leaned back and secured the seat belt. "I understand that his father has requested that he be discharged from the hospital."

Awele's eyes grew wide in surprise before she squinted at him in confusion. "But…I thought he was getting better. I thought he was responding to treatment."

"The malaria has been controlled, but his other ailment remains. It is going to be a long time before he can be cured. The doctors are trying their best, but he appears not to be responding as well as they were hoping he would."

She considered telling him that she knew what the ailment was but decided against it. Instead, she leaned back again, recalling her conversation with Ma Edem about Chibala, the "super" witch doctor. Could Pa Edem's reason for requesting the discharge from hospital be because he wanted to take Edem to Chibala?

The painkillers had eased her aches and pains. The gentle breeze felt refreshing, reducing the perspiration that still gathered in rivulets on her face and neck. Too tired to think, Awele closed her eyes again and drifted off to sleep.

CHAPTER 19

"Come visit me" and "come live with
me" are two different things.

—African proverb

I t had been agreed that the Garuba children would go back to school for the remainder of the school year. There were only four weeks left and Afam had been inclined to let them wait until September to begin the new session, but his mother did not agree, and the children didn't seem to mind. So he booked an appointment and dropped them off at the Montessori Elementary and Secondary School in Port Harcourt on Thursday afternoon to complete the admission tests.

A staff member was chatting with the children when he entered the reception at the agreed pickup time later that afternoon. The boys looked relaxed and comfortable, laughing at something the lady was saying. Their easy rapport could only mean that the tests had gone well. Afam was relieved. He had expected they would be okay, of course, but with the change in curriculum and the new environment, he had been a little worried. He looked around and found Kamdi sitting on a sofa at the far corner of the room. The folded hands across her chest seemed to tell a different story.

They all stopped when they saw him, but it was to the school representative that he directed his question. "How did they do?"

Kamdi's unsmiling, wide-eyed stare reminded him of a lonely puppy.

"Good afternoon, sir. I'm Ifeoma, the school receptionist." The lady stretched out a hand, which he shook. "The principal would like to see you. Please follow me."

He winked at the children before following the receptionist to another room where a spectacled grey-haired man got up from behind a table to shake his hand.

"They did very well," he told Afam. "Each of them is well above the class average in all the subjects. I'm extremely impressed."

"And the girl?"

"Ah yes, the girl. Your niece is a smart young girl. She had one of the best maths scores I have seen on these tests for her grade level, both in speed and accuracy. I think they will be great additions to the school. It's entirely up to you if you want to bring them in this term or wait until September. It won't make any difference to us. We'll accept them any time."

Afam nodded his thanks. He wanted to tell him the children would start immediately, but remembering Kamdi's worried frown, he decided to wait until he had spoken to them before making the commitment.

As they got into the car, he gave them the good news.

"Yes!" John shouted, giving his brother a high five. "Yes!" he exclaimed again. "I told you so, Peter."

"Great!" Peter grinned back.

Afam listened to the two boys comparing notes about the tests and the school amenities they had seen on the tour. He heard laughter in their voices, saw anticipation in their faces, and knew it would be okay for them to start right away. It would be good for them to get out of the compound, meet new people, make new friends, and face new challenges.

"What about you, Kamdi? What do you think? Would you like to attend this school?" Afam asked the quiet girl.

"Yes, sir," her voice was a little more than a whisper. He was driving and could not turn to see her face, but she sounded forlorn, and Afam's heart filled with pity.

"You don't sound very sure," he continued gently. "Are you okay?"

She nodded and looked out of the window. But when he glanced at her through the rearview mirror, he saw a huge tear roll down her cheeks.

Her brothers had seen the tears, too, and Peter rushed to explain.

"It's because the classes are in different buildings, sir. She will be in the elementary wing, while John and I will be in junior secondary. She's not used to being on her own, sir. She has been in our father's class for the past two years, so she's scared to be on her own now."

Afam had not considered this. "Kamdi, is this a big problem? Should we try another school?"

"Why?"

"Because I want you to be comfortable. There are many other schools in Port Harcourt, and if you don't like this one, we can just keep looking until we find the one you like."

The two boys turned to their sister, their excitement waning. The little girl looked from one brother to the other, and more tears rolled down her cheeks. John took her hand and squeezed tight as they waited for her verdict. "Tell Uncle Izuwa what you want, Kamdi. Peter and I won't mind if we cannot attend this Montessori school."

"But you both like it. You just said so."

"Yes, we do. But it won't be fun if you don't like it too. We're a family. As much as we can, we will stay together. You know that's what Pa and Ma would want."

She turned to look at their guardian. He saw her struggling to say the right thing and smiled his encouragement. "Can I change my mind later?"

"Of course," Afam said, stepping on his brake to avoid a woman jaywalking between cars in the slow-moving traffic. The woman was tugging a child in her hand and carrying another on her back. As he waited for them to safely cross the road, he glanced back and held Kamdi's eyes. "Tell you what, you all can attend this school for the four weeks left in the session. If you still don't like it at the end of the term, we will explore other schools. Can you do that?"

She nodded, looking down to break the eye contact. "Would I have to wear the school uniform?"

"Yes, Kamdi." He arched his brows. "Is that a problem?"

She turned red as the next words left her lips. "Would they let me wear my bracelet? It's from my ma and pa. I have to wear it all the time."

Afam glanced at the bracelet. It looked too big on her slim wrist. He had often wondered why she always wore it. He had not realized it was a gift from her parents. "Would you like me to ask for special permission for you?"

"Yes please."

"Then I will. If they say no and we can't work out a compromise, we will just keep looking for another school for next session. Is that a deal?"

Large grateful eyes beamed up at him. "Thank you, Uncle 'Zuwa."

*****

As Afam drove toward his compound, he saw a taxi parked outside his gate. When he saw who was in the taxi, his face stiffened, and he bit down on his lips. Just yesterday, he had told Vickie that their relationship was over and done with. But being Vickie, of course, she had not taken him seriously. So here she was, parked in front of his house, a lazy smile curving the sides of her mouth. When their eyes met, he shook his head slowly in reproof, but her smile only grew wider. With no love lost between his mother and Vickie, it looked like his evening would be anything but the quiet evening he had been envisioning on the drive home.

Conscious of three pairs of curious eyes that followed his gaze toward the taxi, Afam wound down the window on the driver's side and said brightly. "Hey, Vickie, what are you doing here?"

"Your gateman wasn't sure if he should let me in since you were not at home." She pouted, as she stepped out of the taxi and walked toward his car. "I didn't want to argue with him, so I waited. I brought a few gifts for Mommy. Please tell Musa to open the gate so the taxi can come in and off-load the things I have brought."

"Excuse me?"

She smiled again. "I said I came to greet your mother, and I brought a few gifts with me. Can the taxi drive into your compound?"

Afam winced silently. Vickie had to be up to something, or high on something. Wasn't she the one who had called his mother a witch to her face only a few months ago? Did she think his mother had forgotten?

"The taxi can wait outside. Musa and Amadi can bring the stuff into the compound. You didn't have to buy anything for my mother, you know. She is not going to accept them."

Vickie laughed. "Well, I couldn't have come empty-handed to visit her, could I? That would be going against our culture."

He did not buy any of that. She was definitely up to something. Unfortunately for her, she had no idea how determined Phidelia Izuwa could be. But he did, and it would take more than a few gifts for his mother to be impressed or deceived by Vickie. His gaze locked with hers again.

"Don't say I didn't warn you," he muttered.

Vickie's response was an amused, daring smile.

"Uncle Izuwa, we can help Musa to off-load the boot and bring the things inside the house," a young voice offered.

"No, Peter, you will not. Musa and Amadi can bring in whatever needs to be brought into the house."

Vickie heard the exchange and her smile grew wider. "Are the children in the car? Oh, I'm sorry, guys. I didn't realize you were in there. How are you all?"

The children looked at one another questioningly.

"We're fine, ma," Peter answered for them.

Vickie looked at them closer. "Your uncle was right. You seem like a very good boy, Peter. You too, John. And Kamdi, oh my god, what a beautiful girl you are."

The children turned their eyes to their guardian, waiting for introductions.

"They don't know who you are," he told Vickie. "How about we all go in and we can have proper introductions?"

At his signal, Musa opened the gate, and he drove into the compound. It was late afternoon, and the intense heat was gradually dying down. Phidelia, Amadi, and Nneka were on the terrace, cutting *okazi* leaves and peeling *egusi* melon seeds. Afam knew the exact moment his mother recognized Vickie. Her smile froze, and her angry gaze locked with the younger woman's. Afam cleared his throat and braced himself for a stressful evening.

"Ah! Mommy, welcome!" Vickie joyfully exclaimed and ran to kneel at Phidelia's feet. "I'm so happy to see you, ma. It was only on Tuesday that your son told me that you have been around. I would have come to greet you sooner if I had known. I hope he has been taking good care of you."

In response, Phidelia hissed loudly, shook off Vickie's hands from her feet and turned away. Afam winced.

"*Haba* Mommy, it's me—Vickie." She stretched out an arm to touch Phidelia again. "Have you forgotten me, Mommy?"

Phidelia hissed again and shook off the beseeching arms.

"*Tufiakwa!* Who is your mommy?" She spat on the ground. "Go and look for your mother if she's lost. I'm not your mother."

Undeterred, Vickie continued to pout and cajole. "Ah, you're my mommy o! And like a mother, I know you will forgive me for my rudeness the last time you came. Our elders say that foolishness is a child's prerogative, but it does not mean he will be disowned by his parents. Forgive me for my foolishness, ma. I'm very sorry."

"Leave me alone!"

"I know it's because of what happened when you came the other time. I was very rude to you. I have come to ask for your forgiveness, ma. Please give me another chance, ma."

Phidelia stood up and started to gather the plastic containers of peeled *egusi* melon seeds. Nneka helped her to dust off the feather-thin shells from her wrapper before gathering the discarded vegetable stalks into a garbage bag.

"Afam, where are those children? Did the school accept them? Did you register them?"

At this, the children dutifully went to their stepgrandmother and recounted their experience at the Montessori school. They would be starting school on Monday.

"It's not far from here. I think we can walk to the school in thirty minutes or less," Peter told her.

"Why would you do that? I thought they have a school bus. Or did Afam say you will be walking to school?"

"No, ma," Peter hastened to assure her. "He didn't say so. I just assumed that since it is not that far, we can walk."

Phidelia shook her head at him, irritated. "Haven't you heard about all the criminals wandering about town? Or didn't you learn anything from your parents' death? Do you want someone to kidnap you along the way so you can throw my son's life into more chaos than you already have?"

"No, ma. I'm sorry, ma," Peter replied.

The children turned back to their uncle, wide-eyed with confusion and hurt. Kamdi was blinking rapidly, her eyes rolling from side to side, and Afam knew she had not yet overcome her fear of her stepgrandmother.

"*Nne*, that's not true," he protested loudly. "These children have not thrown my life into any kind of chaos."

Phidelia only hissed and retied her outer wrapper.

"It's okay, children." Vickie smiled at the children in sympathy. She reached for John's hand. "You don't have to fear your grandmother. She didn't mean to hurt you. She's not like those evil grandmothers in your children's books. Her bark is far worse than her bite. You'll see that she—"

"Vickie!" Afam remonstrated. She was not making things better. Nor was she fooling anybody with her pretences at commiseration.

"You're the evil woman!" Phidelia's voice rang out in anger. "You're the evil woman who wants to ruin my son's life. But it will not happen, do you hear me? I will not be alive and see you destroy my family. God forbid! Your juju will explode on your head. You will not destroy my son's life, and you will not destroy my grandchildren's lives either."

Phidelia reached out and yanked John's hand from Vickie's grasp. "Leave them alone. Children, go into the house now. Go and wash and get ready for dinner. I don't want any of you to have anything to do with this woman. She's evil. Do you hear me? She's evil. Now go."

The children hesitated only to look to their uncle for permission before rushing into the house.

"Fine girl!" Vickie called just as Kamdi tried to pass by her.

The little girl turned and blinked myopic eyes at her, and Vickie stepped back, raising her hands as if to stop the girl from coming closer. Afam saw fear in Vickie's eyes, although she switched on her bright smile again.

"Your bracelet is very pretty, truly unique. I like it. Where did you get it from?"

Kamdi's lips firmed tighter as she stared at the woman.

"They are my pa and my ma's ashes."

Vickie's hand fell to her side. Shock and fear battled for control of her face.

"Ashes? Did you say ashes?"

Kamdi stared defiantly at her. "Yes. They are my parents' ashes. My auntie scooped ashes from where they died and poured into these small shells on my bracelet. This way, the spirits of my parents are always with me when I wear it."

"Oh. Oh, I'm sorry." Vickie's lips curled in disgust, even as she struggled for self-control.

"Didn't I say you should leave her alone?" Phidelia yelled. "Go to your room, Kamdi. Go with your brothers. Now!"

Kamdi ran.

Just then, Musa and Amadi arrived bearing the foodstuff from the taxi.

"What do you have there?" Phidelia asked her son. "Did you go to the market?"

Vickie smiled with pride as the servants brought in item after item. "Mommy, these are gifts from me. Nothing much, just some rice and beans, yams, plantains, stockfish, a couple of wrappers… I brought them to greet you and to say welcome to Port Harcourt, ma."

Phidelia opened her mouth in shocked dismay. "You brought these for me? Why?"

"Peace offerings, Mommy, atonement for any and every thing I have done that has made you so angry with me. I like your son very much, ma, and I will be very happy for us to be friends, for his sake. Who knows, in future I may even become your daughter-in-law and—"

"Hey, hey, hey!" Phidelia pinched her ear and shook her head. "Don't you have ears? Have you not heard a word of all I've been saying since you came here? I don't want your gifts. I don't need your foodstuff. If I'm hungry and I have nothing to eat, my son will provide for me. I don't need your wrapper and blouses. I can clothe myself. Haven't you heard that I own a boutique? If I don't like the clothes I sell, all I have to do is ask my son, and he will buy what I want. I don't want you to come and greet me. Go away with your witchcraft. My son will not marry you. Go and find another unsuspecting man to bewitch. Your juju will not work here."

Afam bristled with hurt and embarrassment for Vickie, even though he could see how she had brought this upon herself. He knew that her contriteness was not genuine and that any minute now she would take off her veneer of repentance and begin to trade insults with his mother. But when his mother marched into the house, he turned toward her and saw the defeat she could not hide from her face. She wiped the tears rolling down her cheeks and began to sob. Before he could step away, she hurled herself into his arms and started to bawl her eyes out.

CHAPTER 20

Walls have ears.

—African proverb

She was running through the thorny path of a thick forest, and the shadows were chasing her. Their grunting and chanting sounded like slashing knives. Tall and willowy, short and fat, thin and long—shadows of every description followed her. But giant trees and shrubs in the forest blocked her path, and the shadows gained on her. Still, she ran. The path looked familiar, and she realized that somehow, she was running in circles around Magaji estate. She ran past her bungalow, past Edem's bungalow, and straight into the ancestral shrine. Tokumbo stood at the altar, holding her large suitcase, silently willing her to look at her. Awele looked, and gasped, for instead of eyes, her friend had vacant, gaping holes. The chanting of the shadows grew closer, converging on the girls. Long, cold fingers reached Tokumbo as she stood at the altar. Awele launched forward to save her friend, strained toward her, but Tokumbo slipped through her shaking fingers, into the suitcase, and disappeared. The shadows then turned to her. It was dark, she was afraid, but there was no way out.

Awele heard a buzzing in her ear, and her eyes flew open. Heart pounding, she exhaled gratefully. *Thank you, Jesus.* It was a dream; a terrible, frightening but harmless nightmare. She was safe in her room, on her own bed, with no one pursuing her.

Something trickled down her face, and as she lifted her bedsheet to wipe it off, she felt more wetness on the pillow. Gently, she sat up on the bed and realized that her bed sheet was drenched with her sweat. Awele shuddered. This was the third night. Wasn't the malaria supposed to have left by now? *Try this new medication,* Dr. Ben had said. *It heals malaria faster than chloroquine. The only thing is that you may have a few bad dreams but nothing major.*

Yeah, right. *That* was a major nightmare.

It hurt when she sat up—all the blood in her head seemed to immediately flow from her brain to her limbs—so she gently lowered her body back on the bed and laid still. But the ghostly shadows in her nightmare flashed through her mind again. She opened her eyes quickly, blinked repeatedly until they faded away. She checked her phone. It was only a quarter after twelve midnight. There was no way she could sleep through the night on the wet linen. She could either change the sheets or place a towel over it.

But first, her medications. Using only the illumination from her cell phone, she made her way to the living room for the plastic bottles she kept on the coffee table. And just as she uncorked one bottle, she heard the last gasp of her phone battery and groaned for the thick darkness that followed. She turned to feel her way along the wall for the light switch, and as she reached it, her breath caught in shock.

Silhouetted against the dark shivers of her window blinds were those shadows again. This was not a dream. They were real shadows of two people having a conversation just outside her living room. They were standing very close together, whispering. In the stillness of the night and partial illumination of the moon, she recognized her landlord. Her curiosity got the better of her and she quietly knelt down and soundlessly crawled on her carpeted floor toward the window.

"You know, life is so funny," she heard the low voice of Pa Edem. "Years ago, I set boundaries for myself regarding what I could do in all good conscience and what I could not do. This is one of those things I promised myself I would never do."

There was a momentary silence before she heard the sympathetic response from the longer and unfamiliar shadow.

"I know, my friend. I've been through that before. There are many things I have also said to myself that I will never do. But life happens, and a man has to do what he has to do to protect himself and his family."

Awele listened to her heavy breathing. Her heartbeat was pounding so thunderously in her ears that she felt the men outside her window could hear it too. They obviously thought she was not in the house. Why else would they be speaking so freely just by her window?

"In many ways, I feel as though the gods set me up. First, they inflict my son with a disease that only they can cure, and then they turn around and ask me to do the very thing I have sworn never to do in all my life, as the only condition for his healing."

"That is the way of the gods," the stranger's voice said. "They never give us decent choices. We are all pawns in their hands. If it is any consolation to you, my brother, you're not the first person they have asked to make the ultimate sacrifice in exchange for his child's life. And you will not be the last."

Ultimate sacrifice? Awele hunched lower still, praying that they would not hear the breathing that sounded so loud in her own ears.

"I offered them everything under the earth. Everything! Money, animals, land. But Chibala said no. In fact, the high priest got angry. He said that my bargaining with the gods showed I was not serious about getting healing for my son. He said it is the god of the land where Edem went, where he stepped on the juju, that is demanding the sacrifice, and that I have to comply or watch my son die."

"Hmm." Awele heard the stranger click his fingers. "Did they tell you what to do when you have sourced the offering?"

"Oh yes…and it is not pretty."

Pa Edem's voice dropped lower, and his next words were lost on her. But not to his friend, who sounded shocked.

"Are you sure?"

"Absolutely."

"But that means it has to happen here, in your compound!"

"Yes. Unless I can find somewhere else to take Edem to where no one can see us. Normally, the priest accepts the offering in his temple and makes the sacrifice on behalf of the petitioner. But in this case, they say the gods require him to prepare the offering by himself, and this is something only he can do."

Awele suspected that the clicking tongue she heard was from the stranger. They were silent for a while before she heard him ask, "And how long did they give you?"

"Seven days from yesterday, I'm already one day short. If we don't deliver the offering in exactly six days, Edem will die."

"Ah, my brother, what will you do?"

"This is why I have called you. I know you have the ear of Emerole the hunter. The chief priest said I should talk to him, that he will help me find what I need."

"Hmm, I doubt that. Emerole has retired from this business. His late brother's son has come to live with him, a young man who goes to church and reads the Bible. He has succeeded in giving Emerole a guilty conscience."

Pa Edem grunted. "Impossible. That doesn't make sense."

"In a way, it does. No one wants to go to hell, you know. If such a place exists, Emerole will surely burn. His hands are not clean by any means."

"Ah, my brother. I don't care. All I know is that I cannot lose my son. You have to help me. Talk to him. Beg him for me. Tell him that I am ready to pay anything for his help."

"*Chei,* my brother, if we don't have Emerole, or people like him to help us, how can we appease the gods?"

"Exactly!" Pa Edem's voice rose in his distress. "He has to help me. I don't want my son to die. Can't you try, my brother?"

"Shh…don't panic. I'll call him. And if he says no, we will find someone else."

The stranger dropped his voice lower, and Awele could not catch his next words, but Pa Edem's dismissal was clear. "You mean my tenant, the youth corper? Oh no, don't worry about her. She's sick in the hospital. She's not at home."

"Ah, that is good to know." The stranger sounded relieved. "Our people say that walls have ears. No one should hear what we have just discussed."

"Of course. Even Ma Edem will not hear of it. You cannot trust women."

Silence. More whispers. Awele felt her breathing pick up again as she listened to the fading footsteps and the creaking of the estate gate as it opened and closed after the stranger.

What were they talking about, she wondered? What sacrifice? What *ultimate* sacrifice?

CHAPTER 21

*The dog I bought bit me, the
fire I kindled burned me.*

—African proverb

K amdi looked up from her seat in front of the class and fixed her eyes on a spot on the blackboard. She was dressed in a pink pinafore and matching beret, the temples of her thick-rimmed glasses held tightly behind her ears. Although the children's admission had been arranged in three short days, they had been able to start on Monday without any major incident. The deal breaker would have been the bracelet, which the principal had refused for her to wear to school. At Afam's suggestion, Nneka had curled the bracelet multiple times, held the coils together with a thread, and ran a thin rope through them to transform it into a necklace. This was approved by the principal, and she now wore the necklace under her pinafore. Kamdi liked the feel of the shells resting over her heart. No one could see it, and no one would ask those embarrassing questions anymore.

"What's the matter?" her class teacher asked. Kamdi had not heard Miss Pelly approach her desk. "Do you understand what you're supposed to do? Do you need help with anything?"

"I've finished," she replied and heard a student at the back burst out in subdued laughter. Kamdi took a deep breath and held her head high. She would not give in to the temptation to glance back despite the nervous tension that rose in her stomach.

"Are you sure?" Miss Pelly asked. "It's been only twenty minutes. You still have thirty more minutes to complete the test. Do you want to look over your work?"

"I've finished," she repeated and heard another muffled laughter. They were making fun of her, and she decided she did not care. She found her classmates very unfriendly. They laughed at her Hausa accent, they called her "oyibo," and they made fun of her unwillingness to go outside in the hot sun during recess. She had also seen the way some of the teachers looked at her, as though she was dumb because of her skin pigmentation. Moreover, in the week she had been in the school, she had not seen any other albino child, so she knew she was something of a rarity, an object for unabashed curiosity and endless speculation.

"Shh!" Miss Pelly warned the snickering students. Kamdi handed in her paper and watched as the teacher's eyes scanned her answers.

Uncle Izuwa had taken care to plan a seamless transition for them into the Montessori school. A vehicle and driver arrived to pick them up at seven thirty in the morning to take them to school and came back for them at ten-to-four in the afternoon. Auntie Nneka had their dinner ready when they got back, and Grandma Phidelia would nag them to complete their homework as soon as they were done eating.

"This is incredible!" Miss Pelly's eyes rounded in wonder. "Did you write all these just now?"

"Yes, I did."

"Wow! You really do know your math facts. Congrats. This is excellent." Then she raised her voice louder and looked around the class, "One hundred percent score achieved in half the test time."

Kamdi wanted to tell her that her father had taught her math facts and that she knew them like the back of her hands. But she bit her lips and kept quiet. She missed her father. When she finally looked round, the students who were not frowning at their answer sheets or chewing the butts of their pencils were staring at her!

"May I be excused, Miss Pelly? I need to ease myself."

"Of course,'" the woman beamed at her. "And you can take an early recess. You have earned it."

Kamdi thanked her quietly and left the classroom.

From the washroom, she went to the playground. That first day, on Monday, she had come out to play on the swings but the long queue of students waiting for their turns, the hot sun, and the din of children everywhere on the field had been too much for her senses. She had found a shade under an umbrella tree instead and had sat there until recess was over. She sat under the same shade during recess on Tuesday, Wednesday, and again on Thursday.

Now she looked at her watch. It was twenty minutes until recess. She glanced around. There was no student out on the playground yet. She had twenty minutes until pandemonium would break out again with all the kids on the field. She had twenty minutes to do anything she wanted. She could play on the swing for twenty minutes, do the monkey bars for twenty minutes, or even go down the slides—all at her own pace—for twenty whole minutes!

She looked around again as she started toward the swings. This school was much bigger than her former school. In Maiduguri, they had attended a state primary school for elementary one to junior secondary. Compared to this school, that was child's play. This one had more buildings, more students, more teachers, and a huge athletics field that separated the elementary block from the junior and secondary school blocks.

She was not bothered that there would be no one to give her a push on the swing. It did not really matter. Long ago, her father had explained to her about gravity and how to twist and turn her body until the swing would get into a rhythmic grove, and the pendulum would start moving up and down. Now she sat on the swing and closed her eyes, trying to feel him—the way his strong hands would lift her up on the swing and push her high in the sky while she screamed in sheer delight. After a few minutes, she twisted her body to the correct angle, first lunged backward, then forward, and gradually, as the swing picked up speed and momentum, she smiled happily and let herself go!

By the time the recess bell rang, she was still on the swing. As soon as the gates opened and pandemonium released the horde of kids into the playground, she quickly stepped down and found her usual place in the shade of the umbrella tree.

"Did you really get one hundred percent in the math test?"

She did not recognize the tall girl that stood looking down at her. She was not in her class.

"Who told you?

"Chinelo. She's in your class. She said Miss Pelly told everyone that you got one hundred percent."

Kamdi folded her hands across her chest and waited for the next comment. More girls had come to where they stood, listening to the conversation.

"Did you cheat? Even I found the test difficult, and I'm the smartest maths student in elementary three."

Kamdi gasped.

"Of course, I did not cheat. I'm a Christian. I do not cheat."

"Relax. You don't need to be so proud. I'm also a Christian, and I sometimes cheat."

"Well, I don't."

The attentive crowd broke out in laughter.

"Imagine that!" someone announced. "Christians who cheat in exams. They are both going straight to hell!"

"Amen!" More laughter. "God will punish them!" Kamdi kept a steady gaze across the field.

"My name is Cecilia. Is your name really Candy?"

The tall girl was persistent.

"No, it's Kamdi, short for Otuakamdi."

Cecilia thought about it for a full two seconds before making a face. "That's too long. I like Candy better. It makes everyone think you are as sweet as candy. I wish my name was Candy. My mom says I eat too much candy and that's why I have teeth problem."

Kamdi said nothing. As long as she didn't call her *oyibo*, she was fine with any variation of her name the girl fancied. But she wished Cecilia would just go away with her friends and leave her alone.

"I like maths. I am very good with numbers. My father says I have a computer brain. I remember many numbers. When I grow up, I want to be an inventor. What do you want to be when you grow up?"

Kamdi chewed at her thumb and looked away. By now, the other kids had scattered in different directions, leaving just the two of them. "I don't know."

The other students were now in clusters, some on the swings, some on the slides, and some were playing hopscotch on the pavement. She liked hopscotch. It was still early days for her, but hopefully the girls would soon invite her to play with them.

"Are you really a Christian?" she asked before she could stop herself.

"Yes." Cecilia nodded. "But I'm not a good Christian. My mother says I shouldn't cheat, and I shouldn't tell lies, but it's easy for me to lie when I get into trouble and to cheat when I don't want to lose in a test or a competition. I would rather cheat and score one hundred percent than be honest and fail. I guess God will just have to forgive me if he wants me to go to heaven. My mother says he always forgives everybody who apologizes to him."

Kamdi opened her mouth wide in horror. "But you cannot do that. God is not stupid. He knows when we are genuinely sorry and when we are not. If you say sorry when you don't mean it, he will know and he will not forgive you."

"How do you know? Are you God?"

"I'm not, but it's in the Bible somewhere."

"I don't like to talk about it. Hey, let's go play hopscotch with the girls."

Kamdi hesitated. She noticed that some of the girls were waiting for Cecilia.

"No, that's okay. You go. I'll watch from here." She had been in the sun too long already. Any more exposure and her skin would begin to itch and she would scratch, and it would break into red patches. "I'll play with you next week."

Another bell rang in the distance, and the junior secondary classes began to stream out for their recess. Kamdi recognized her brothers in the middle of some other boys. One of them had a soccer ball, and she did not have to guess where they were headed. She was happy for them. They were having fun, making friends, and enjoying the school. But she would not stay after this term. She would ask Uncle Izuwa to look for a smaller school, just for her. No need to move her brothers. For sure, it would be lonely without Peter and John, but she would just have to try and cope.

"Hey, Oyibo!"

Kamdi turned to see one of the staff from the school office beckoning to her. She had to pretend that she did not care about the moniker. Pursing her lips, she got up from where she was seated and met the woman halfway across the field.

"Come. There's someone in the office to see you."

"Someone to see me. Are you sure?"

"What do you mean, am I sure? Are you questioning me? Come!" said the woman, whose badge read MRS. IFEOMA NWOKORIE, Receptionist. Kamdi remembered her from the evening they had come for their admission tests.

Mrs. Nwokorie grabbed her by the hand and pulled impatiently. "Follow me. Your aunt is here. Your grandmother has fallen sick, and your uncle is with her in the hospital. He wants you and your brothers to come immediately. Hurry up."

Kamdi's heart began to pound in her ears. *Another death? Please, Lord. Why do people have to die?*

The woman escorted her to her classroom and had words with Miss Pelly. There were no students around. Kamdi packed her stuff into her backpack, hurled it across her shoulder, and quickly followed the receptionist to the main office.

She did not recognize anyone at the reception office. Ifeoma Nwokorie looked around, too, apparently not seeing the person she was looking for. A little girl, maybe two or three years old, holding onto her mother's hand stared wide-eyed at Kamdi. The woman was talking on her cell phone and didn't bat an eyelid at the sight of Kamdi.

"Madam, can I help you?" Mrs. Nwokorie asked.

The woman turned from her phone for a second.

"Thanks. I'm here to pick up my daughter. She has a dentist appointment in thirty minutes, which I totally forgot about. Your colleague has gone to get her for me."

Another staff whom Kamdi had seen at the reception several times this week hurried into the office.

"Sorry about the delay, madam," she addressed the woman. "Where is she?"

"She's gathering her things and will be here shortly. Please exercise a little patience."

The woman nodded and resumed her phone conversation.

Ifeoma turned to her front desk colleague, "Where that woman wey come to pick up the oyibo come go now?"

"She got tired of waiting for you to bring her. She phoned the secondary school office from here, and they said she could come over immediately for the brothers. But she left her driver and car outside. She said he should pick the *oyibo* and meet her and the boys in front of the JSS admin block."

"Did she sign her out?" Ifeoma asked, flipping through a register on the counter. She saw what she needed and hurriedly led Kamdi outside.

Kamdi counted seven vehicles lined along the loading bay. As they stood wondering which car they were supposed to go to, the driver of a brown SUV stepped out, cigarette in hand, and signaled to them. He opened the back seat of the vehicle and motioned for her to get in. But Kamdi took one look at the driver, smelled the cigarette smoke, and stopped short. She looked up at the receptionist.

"Where is the auntie? Where are my brothers?"

Mrs. Nwokorie turned to the driver. "Where your madam come go?"

"See," he pointed to a woman some distance away. "Na im dey waka go for yonder."

Although she used her hand as a shield from the glare of the sun, Kamdi couldn't see that far ahead. Besides, there were many women in the direction he was pointing.

"She say she no fit wait, say make I bring the girl come meet her for the other side," the driver replied, confirming what

Mrs. Nwokorie's colleague had said. But Kamdi held on to the receptionist.

"I'll wait for my brothers," she stated.

The driver lashed out. "What? Please, no just waste my time. Just get in and let's go. Oga said I should bring all of you to the hospital quick-quick. Your grandmother is about to die, and you are here doing *sme-sme*, stretching your neck like a peacock. Get in now and don't just waste my time."

Ifeoma Nwokorie looked from Kamdi to the driver. The girl's hand in hers tightened. "You can't blame her for refusing to follow you if she doesn't know you. And I think she's right. You go and bring the others, and she will join you. I'll take her back to the office. Call me when you pick them."

"Haba, madam! I don't have the time for all this rigmarole. If I leave here now, I'm not coming back. *Oga* Izuwa will not like it when I tell him you refused to release her to me. If na ID card you wan see, look at it here," he whipped up a card from his jeans trouser.

"Mr. Driver, look here. Don't raise your voice at me. You have your job. I have mine. You do your own anyhow you like it, but you cannot tell me how to do my own. I can't let you just—"

"Ifeoma! Ifeoma!" a voice called from inside the school. They turned. The second receptionist, looking panicked, was running toward them. "Supervisor is on the phone. She said it's urgent."

"What? She's back? I didn't think…did she say…?"

"You better come now. Hurry!"

Kamdi's hand tightened, but Ifeoma shook her off.

"*Oyibo*, sorry. I have to go for a meeting now."

The woman who had been waiting for her daughter at the reception came out. Kamdi was surprised to see Cecilia with her. The other girl stopped and gave her a wide grin and a wave as she followed her mother to the car parked directly behind the brown SUV. "See you on Monday!" she called to Kamdi. "I have to go to the dentist for checkup! I told you, too much candy!"

Kamdi waved back.

"*Oyibo*, I'm sorry, but you have to go with the driver. I have to attend to an emergency." Mrs. Ifeoma Nwokorie nudged her forward, practically pushed her into the car and hurried back into the school building.

As the driver got in the car and drove out slowly from the school, toward the Junior Secondary administration building, Kamdi looked back to see Cecilia still waving to her from the front passenger seat of her mother's car.

*****

At 3.50 p.m., Peter and John met their driver at the designated meeting point and waited for Kamdi to show up. When she did not, they got into the car and drove to the elementary school to see what was holding her up. The school bus had already left, most of the students with it. Those who did not go in the bus and were still waiting for their parents to pick them up were very few. Peter got out of the car and ran to the reception just as the two receptionists were packing up for the day.

"Can I help you?" one of them asked, turning from the computer monitor she was shutting down.

"Yes please, I am looking for my sister. I was wondering if you've seen her."

"The *oyibo*?"

Peter frowned. "Her name is Kamdi. Kamdi Garuba."

"But she's gone."

"Gone where?"

"Your uncle sent someone to pick her up during recess." The receptionist clicked on the shutdown button and reached for her handbag. "The woman said your grandmother is in the hospital. She was coming to pick you and your brother too. What happened? Why didn't you go with her?"

Peter shook his head. "Nobody came for us at recess. My uncle's driver is here to take us home. He didn't say anything about my grandma being ill."

The woman stopped rummaging in her handbag to stare him full in the face.

"Are you sure?"

"Yes, ma." He nodded. "I'm sure. You can come and speak to the driver yourself."

Mrs. Ifeoma Nwokorie's eyes grew wider as she starred at Peter's face and knew that he was telling the truth. Panic seized her.

"Oh my god!" she exclaimed. "Oh, my god! What have I done? What have I done?"

CHAPTER 22

When there is no enemy within, the ene-
mies without cannot hurt you.

—African proverb

For everyone in Afam Izuwa's home, it was a long night, tense with fear and frustration. Nneka sobbed incessantly into her wrapper, sniffing and hiccupping. Amadi kept close to his master, offering bits of advice that rang hollow with helplessness. Phidelia refused her dinner and sat outside on the garden chair all evening, eyes closed, hand on her breasts, heaving, and muttering incoherent words. Peter and John went straight to their room from school, and Afam could hear their young voices alternately wailing and praying for their sister's safe return.

Afam did not have time to dwell on his own emotions that night, but the more he tried to make sense of the events leading to Kamdi's disappearance, the angrier and more helpless he felt. He was angry with the school for their ineffective security protocols, angry with himself for not listening to the instincts that wanted the children to wait out the remainder of the school year, angry because he had not listened to Kamdi's reservations about the school, and angry because he had not adequately warned the children about the dangers of following strangers to anywhere. Angry. Helpless. And totally clueless about what to do next.

Okee had some connection with the police, and they had lodged a missing person report late that evening. The officers at the police station promised to get in touch, and true to their word, two unmarked SUVs bearing police detectives arrived Afam's compound just before midnight and began questioning the household.

Two officers questioned his driver, Amadi, and Nneka; two others interviewed Peter and John; and the others scoured the compound.

Afterward, the police chief called Afam and Phidelia to the living room. He confirmed that his men had picked up Mrs. Ifeoma Nwokorie and taken her to the police station for questioning. He then invited them to tell him all they could about their missing child.

"Remind me again, how this child came into your care?" he prompted.

"We have gone through this many times, Officer," Afam's voice was laced with impatience.

"Yes, yes, I understand." He clicked on the tape recorder he had placed on the table. "But this is for the records."

"She's my niece."

"But you'd never heard about her until five weeks ago?"

"That's right. My sister and her husband died in a terror attack in Maiduguri, and the children were brought to live with me five weeks ago."

"When was the last time you spoke to your late sister?"

"What does this have to do with the missing child?"

"Please answer my question, sir."

"I don't remember exactly what day and on what occasion, but it was before her death."

"Did you know about the albino child before your sister's death?"

"No, sir, but I am happy to take care of my sister's children."

"Okay," the police chief said slowly. "Just bear with me while I think aloud for a minute. Now, according to you, sir, the child is eight years old...you spoke to your sister before her death, but she never told you about her children...or that she had a daughter who was an albino...and...um, you have not seen your sister for over six years. In other words, you were not close to your sister. Did you not find it strange then, to be suddenly given charge of three children you did not even know existed?"

Afam shrugged. "It is what it is, sir. It is the truth."

"Officer," Phidelia's raspy voice broke in impatiently, "with all these up-and-down questions, are you trying to imply that my son has something to do with the disappearance of my granddaughter?"

"Madam, I have not said anything of the sort. Are you trying to imply that he is involved?"

"What?" her voice rose before she toned it down, as though suddenly realizing that she was in the presence of the police. "No, Officer, I never said anything of the sort."

"Then stop interrupting so I can get on with my interrogation!" he warned sharply. Phidelia let out a loud snort and bit down her retort.

"But you must admit that he fits the perfect profile," the officer continued, addressing her in a voice that was a notch mellower.

"Fit the perfect profile for what, sir?"

The police chief's smile did not reach his eyes. "Well now, let's see what we have here, an ambitious young man anxious to make quick money and grow his business. He wouldn't be the first young man to visit a witch doctor for some help along the way to financial utopia, would he? And we know what witch doctors do with body parts of albino people."

"I can assure you, sir," Afam spoke through clenched teeth, suppressing the anger that rose like bile in his throat, "that I am not involved in anything of the sort. I do not believe in juju. I am not involved in any juju. I love my niece and my nephews very much, and I will never hurt or harm them in any way."

"Very well said, sir," the police chief dismissed. "I'm sorry, but in twenty years, I have seen too many of these things to believe even one word of what you just said. I can only go with evidence, and the evidence we have uncovered so far tells me otherwise."

"What do you mean? What evidence?"

He shook his head slowly. "My men have uncovered evidence of occult practice in this compound."

Phidelia's eyes widened in disbelief. "God forbid! What occult practice? My son is not involved in any occult o!"

"If you say so, madam, then it must be true. However, there is someone in this household involved in the occult because outside, under a tree in this compound, there is a wooden box bearing fetish objects and covered with fetish symbols all over it, and unless you can convince me otherwise, that is occult material."

"I don't believe it."

"Very well, you just follow me."

His officers led the way. Their flashlights provided extra illumination to the outside lights in the compound. Afam and Phidelia followed. Amadi and Nneka, along with the children, also followed, albeit at a respectable distance. The officers stopped under the big avocado tree, which stood several yards from the elevated flower garden. Someone had cleared a pile of dried leaves under the tree to reveal a white box shaped like a small wooden coffin. Afam guessed it was about one-foot-long, six inches wide and six inches tall. One of the officers poked at it with a stick, and a strong smell exuded from the tiny coffin. Their prodding disturbed some large flies perching on the coffin, and they began to buzz around. Peter's hand reached for his brother's.

"I want to see what is inside the box. I want to know what is producing this foul odor."

"Open it!" The police chief directed his officer.

"Me, sir?" The officer's voice shook, his eyes grew wide.

"Who else?"

"I think say you mean Officer Kemba, sir."

"Me?" that officer protested. "He didn't tell me. Na you him say make you open am, no be me."

"Me, sir?" The first officer sniffed. "Oga, I no fit oh! Make them open am, sir. Make the person wey get am open the coffin by himself."

"What is this?" their boss reproached them. "You are afraid to open the box?"

"No be so, sir. Only say I no dey put my hand for juju. I'm sorry, sir."

"Hmm, okay." Their boss nodded. "I understand."

He turned to the members of the household gathered at the scene. "You all heard my officers. They will not touch your juju. So, if you know you are the one that placed this mini coffin here, step forward now and open it."

No one spoke. No one moved. Nervous fear slithered through the assembly. After a few minutes, Afam turned impatiently to Amadi. "Get me a rag from the kitchen."

"For what?" Phidelia screamed at her son.

"What do you think? To open the box, of course."

"God forbid! Did you keep it there? Is it yours?"

"No, I didn't. But it's in my compound, and we're just wasting time here. A child is missing, for goodness sake. We need to find her quickly instead of standing about and trying to cut grass with plastic knives. I don't know what this has to do with anything, but if the police chief wants the box open and nobody wants to do it, I'll do it. We need to find Kamdi and bring her home."

"Over my dead body will you touch this box today," Phidelia insisted, standing in his way. Afam held up both hands, moving back. "They said the owner of the juju should open it, and it's not you."

The police chief looked at mother and son for a full minute before turning to the assembled audience.

"Listen up, everyone. I have been in this business for over twenty years. In those years, I have seen many kidnap cases, and I can assure you that in ninety percent of the cases, the perpetrators are usually not strangers to the victims. They know themselves. It's like the good book says, a man's enemies are often members of his own household."

Silence as they all listened, punctuated by Phidelia's heavy breathing.

"All of you here have said the young girl is bright and intelligent. Do you think she would have followed a stranger?"

More silence, some shook their heads.

"Someone she knew came to the school and picked her up, someone she trusted. I want all of you to think hard and help us find that person. She is an albino child, and you all know what witch doctors do with albinos. If you want to see her alive again, you must speak up immediately. Time is of the essence here. In the meantime, if I cannot find out who brought this box into this compound, I will arrest Mr. Izuwa this night and take him to the police station for more interrogation."

A collective gasp went up from the crowd. Everyone started to speak at once in fearful denial. Afam was not sure whether to be angry, to laugh, or to be serious. But he had an idea.

"Musa!" he called out above the din.

"Who is Musa?" the police chief asked.

Ignoring him, Afam called to his security guard again.

When Musa emerged from his post, Afam went after him angrily. "You are the gateman. Nobody comes in or out of this compound without your knowledge. Who brought this box into this compound?"

"Sir, I swear, sir, *walahi talahi*, e no be me."

"Then who did? Who was it? Don't tell me the spirits brought it here by magic because I will not buy it. Who put that box under this tree? Who covered it with leaves?"

"Oga, na...na madam, sir. Na she bring am come. She say make I help her bury the box under the tree. I no get shovel, sir. Na im make I never dig ground bury am since."

"Which madam? Your wife?" he asked incredulously.

"Not my wife, sir. Na your own madam, sir—Madam Vickie. That day, when she come visit your mama for night, na im she bring am come. As she dey wait for you to come back, sir, na im she carry am for bag come meet me for inside my security house. She give me money, sir. She say make I help am bury the box under the tree for night. E never even tey...na just last week when she been come, sir. But as I no get shovel..."

His words threw the crowd into shock and confusion. Everyone stared at Musa, thinking he had to be lying. But Afam remembered Vickie's reaction when she saw Kamdi and the fear she had been unable to cover up when she had called on his mother. Could it be true? His mother and Okee had warned him that she was into the occult, but he had rejected the idea.

"Ah!" Phidelia smote her breast. "I should have known it was her. Did I not tell you that woman is a dangerous, wicked witch? I told you, but you wouldn't listen to me."

The chief of police turned his attention from Phidelia to Afam and back again.

"A man's enemies are often members of his own household," he murmured with a humorless smile. "Who is this Vickie—your girlfriend?"

The police officers eventually left with Vickie's contact details and photographs. They took photos of the box containing the fetish and warned everyone about tampering with evidence.

It was a very long night.

After the police troop left, Afam's thoughts dwelled on Kamdi and dread twisted in his stomach. Where was she? Was she frightened? Confused? Had she been hurt, beaten, raped, or even killed on the altars of a witch doctor? But how could Vickie have done it? She was already back in Lagos. She had left soon after that disastrous visit to his home, and he had spoken to her in Lagos. Was she back in Port Harcourt? Could she have kidnapped Kamdi? Would she really harm that poor innocent girl?

He took Peter and John by the hand and led them back to the sitting room. The boys stared at him, but he could not think of anything to say that would ease the fearful tension he could see in their faces.

"Let's not assume the worst now," he told Peter. The boy's eyes were bright with unshed tears, his lips quivered, and he was shaking.

"Auntie Vickie," his voice shook. "She...she is a good woman, isn't she? She wouldn't harm Kamdi, would she?"

"We will not jump to any hasty conclusions," he told the boy. "We're not even sure she was the one that kidnapped her. Let's just concentrate on making sure your sister comes back to us safe and sound."

But even as he said that, he wondered whom he was trying to convince that Kamdi would be back. His voice lacked conviction.

Blinking back tears, the boy nodded. "She'll come back... I know she will be back...I..."

"Of course, she will. I will do everything in my power to bring her home."

Peter's voice was laced with polite urgency. "Uncle, you don't understand."

Something in his tone caused Afam to stop talking and listen.

"God will fight for her. He always does."

"What do you mean?"

Peter swallowed before he continued. "When she was a baby, she almost died. Her real father wanted to kill her because of her skin color. He said she would bring him bad luck. So, he sold her to a witch doctor. But on the day they were to pick her up, her mother ran away with her and brought her to a church. The pastor called the police to arrest the men, and they were put in prison. But then her family still blamed her for her father's imprisonment and did not want anything to do with her. Later, our mother and father went to the orphanage and brought her home, and she became our sister."

Afam listened, careful not to distract the boy. He heard his mother suck in a deep breath and knew she was also listening to the conversation. All these days, he had been wasting his time trying to reach Binta for answers about Kamdi's parentage. He could have simply asked the boys. Amadi was locking up for the night, but his eyes were fastened on the boy, and he was also listening intently. Nneka sat on a dining chair, her arms crossed over her heart.

"How old was she when your parents brought her home?"

"She was still a baby. They adopted her and changed her name to Garuba."

"Her real father later died in prison," John added, drawing another deep breath from Phidelia. Afam glanced at her face and knew she was thinking that the child had indeed brought bad luck to her family. But what kind of father tries to sell his own daughter to someone who will kill and use her body parts for ritual sacrifices?

"Then, when she was two years old, she was kidnapped at the market," Peter continued with grim determination. "Mama put her on the ground briefly to greet someone, and when she turned around, Kamdi was gone."

"Gone?"

"Kidnapped. The whole market joined to look for her, but nobody knew what happened. She didn't use to cry a lot as a baby, so nobody was surprised that she hadn't made a sound. But later, after she was found, it was discovered that her kidnapper had drugged her as soon as she snatched her away."

Amadi stood like a statue, listening. Tears were rolling down Nneka's eyes.

"How did they find her?" Phidelia asked.

"God saved her again." John replied simply.

The adults waited for more explanation.

"A woman had picked her up when our mother wasn't looking. She drugged her, folded her in a wrapper, and tucked her into a basket. Kamdi was very small as a child. The woman jumped on an *okada* motorcycle taxi and took off with the driver. The driver went too fast, and the motorcycle fell into a deep pothole. The basket fell from the woman's hand, and Kamdi fell out. The *okada* driver realized that this was the albino that had been kidnapped from the market, so he raised an alarm and the police came and arrested the woman."

Phidelia lifted a hand over her mouth. Her eyes were wide with shock. Afam swallowed to dislodge the lump that seemed to have taken root in the middle of his throat.

"The woman said she was barren and that a witch doctor had told her to bring an albino for sacrifice as a condition for her to conceive," John explained. "But now she is in prison. All the people that tried to harm Kamdi ended up harming themselves. My father said her angels are always watching over her. If Auntie Vickie tries to harm Kamdi, God will deal with her o! Hm, she should not try it!"

Afam was glad that no one could read his mind. Had he really been worrying about how to comfort these children? They were the ones providing the comfort for the adults, and the hope that maybe all was not lost regarding their little sister. How could these children be so weak and yet so strong? How did they grow such strong faith?

"We even have a saying in our family that *he who keeps Kamdi neither sleeps nor slumbers.* It's in Psalm 121. My father said it was written specially for her. We call it a Song for Kamdi. We all memorized the verses of that psalm when we were little, we can all recite it from heart."

Afam fixed his eyes on the intricate design of the grey rug under his feet. Nneka was weeping openly now. Amadi sneezed into his shirt. Even Phidelia's jaws were quivering.

"Please would you all pray with John and me?" Peter asked around tearfully.

For all his brave words, Afam could see he was still a little boy, still afraid for his sister's safety.

"The God that saved her from her father's evil plan and from the wicked barren woman can still save her." His voice broke. "Please pray with us that she will be found safe and sound. Please pray that God's presence will be with her so she will not be afraid."

The four adults came together and joined hands with the boys in the sitting room. They bowed their heads as the two boys started to recite Psalm 121:

I will lift my eyes to the hills. From where does my help come? My help comes from the Lord who made heaven and earth. He will not let your foot be moved; He who keeps you will not slumber. Behold, he who keeps Israel will neither slumber nor sleep. The Lord is your keeper; The Lord is your shade on your right hand. The sun shall not strike you by day nor the moon by night. The Lord will keep you from all evil; He will keep your life. The Lord will keep your going out and your coming in, from this time forth and forevermore.

CHAPTER 23

A child that says his mother will
not sleep will also not sleep.

—African proverb

Somewhere between the haze of sleeping and waking, a young man saw the subdued lights of a vehicle come to a stop in front of the security gate to his house and heard the opening and closing of car doors and the murmur of voices. It took him a moment to rush out of his room to scoop up the growling puppy and peep through the keyhole to see if he recognized the people speaking with the gateman. His uncle, aunt, and his cousins had long retired for the day. Their rooms were upstairs, but his was on the ground floor, so he had easy access to every noise from the security gate.

"Shh, BJ." He motioned to the yapping dog. "Shh..."

The dog licked the hand he put over its mouth and whined again, his ears standing, and his tiny whiskers straight and alert. The dog was small and couldn't bark, which was why they had adopted him as a pet instead of a guard dog. But when he was upset about something, his whining was almost as good as a bark.

The young man heard the gateman ask the visitors to identify themselves.

"MoBoy and Area Scatter are here to see Mr. Emerole," he heard a voice say. The gate was only a few feet from the front door, so he could hear them clearly. And since it was already well past midnight, everywhere was quiet, so that the voices carried far.

"Come back tomorrow," the gateman replied. "Oga Emerole, he don sleep. Oga madam, he don sleep. Everybody don sleep."

"Go and wake Emerole up," the visitor ordered. "Tell him it's an emergency."

The young man heard his uncle coming downstairs.

"Go to bed now," he was directed. "I will see to the visitors."

"Yes, sir." He nodded, gave a bow, and turned toward his room. He heard his uncle open the front door and direct the gateman to open for them to drive in. Quickly, he ran to his window and peeped through the curtains to see what was happening. One of the men stood talking to his uncle while the second drove the car into the compound and parked on the right side of the security house, next to Emerole's minivan.

They exchanged pleasantries as Emerole led them from the security gate toward the loud, vibrating generators in the backyard, where the young man could not overhear their conversation. But he remembered that there was a bathroom close to the generator house and that he could hear them from there. Before he could change his mind, he ran toward the bathroom. *Maybe my uncle is in trouble*, he thought.

He had forgotten about BJ until the dog jumped down from his arms and tore out of the house through the partially opened front door. The young man had no choice but to quietly go after him to bring him in. He knew his uncle would be furious if he saw him outside, so he moved quietly.

He found the dog whining behind the visitors' vehicle.

From the soft hues of the streetlights, he looked closely at the car and saw that the trunk was slightly ajar; it hadn't been shut properly. On impulse, he lifted the lid up slightly so he could slam it shut. It was then he heard a muffled whimper coming from inside. He opened the lid a bit higher and saw what looked like a big *garri* bag, tied at one end with a rope. The whimpering sound was coming from inside the bag. He leaned closer. Something in the sack seemed to be moving, straining. Probably a goat, tied up and left in the sack. That could have been why they had left the lid of the boot slightly open—to allow the goat to breathe in some fresh air. If that was the case, then there was probably no need to shut it tight. He would leave it just as they had left it—slightly open. He finally caught the puppy and put a leash around his neck. As he turned to return to the main house, he glanced at the vehicle again and realized he had left the trunk much wider than he had found it. He had to close the lid a bit more to return it to its original angle. He got to the boot and lifted the lid just as a sudden streak of light beamed from the headlights of a passing vehicle. Were his eyes deceiving him or did he see a tiny human foot straining from a rip in the sack? Intrigued, he opened the lid higher, followed the contours of the sack, and it led him to the face of a child at the other end, a child whose head hung limply on the spare tire, and whose body, from the neck down, was folded into the large *garri* sack. As the beam slowly faded, he heard voices and realized the men were coming back to the car. Heart beating like drums in his ears, he hastily shut the trunk, grabbed the dog, and swiftly ran into the house. Shocked and confused, he stood at the foot of the stairs for countless minutes. He watched the men open the trunk as they continued their discussion, which had now turned into a subdued argument. The last words he heard were of his uncle berating the visitors. "If you know how to wake her up, you'd better start now. I gave you clear instructions—a live female, not a dead female. What do you expect me to do now? I am not a miracle worker. I cannot raise the dead to life."

Long after the men had entered their vehicle and left and his uncle had locked up and retired to his bedroom, the young man lay on his bed wondering if he had dreamed up the whole incident.

CHAPTER 24

The police is your friend.

—the Nigerian Police promo

The first thing Afam noticed as he approached the police station on Monday morning was the inventory of abandoned vehicles and motorcycles that littered the front yard. The station looked like an unkempt mechanic workshop. It was only about nine thirty in the morning, yet radios were blaring from different parts of the yard, and uniformed officers were milling around the bread and *akara* vendors who had taken positions beside the abandoned vehicles. One of the vehicles was a flatbed, and some officers were using its skeletal remains as a huge dining table. Afam observed the way the officers had arranged the vehicles to look like a fence for their makeshift open-air mess hall.

A stern-looking policeman on guard at the entrance of a building marked "Administration" spotted him and yelled, "You there! Who are you looking for?"

"The DPO—Mr. Kwaku," he replied. "He sent for me."

He was directed to the charge room and told to wait to be called. He sat on a worn bench beside the entrance, switched on his phone and scrolled through the avalanche of emails with tips and offers of help from many people that had flooded his phone since Friday. Most people agreed that this was not a typical abduction. If it were, the kidnappers would have contacted him by now, demanding for ransom. It was an abduction for ritual sacrifice, many concluded, and the child may never be found. He read again the email from Chief Martins, his father's former business partner. He had heard about the kidnapping from his wife, who had heard about it from Afam's mother. He wanted Afam to call him immediately. He lived in Abuja, he said, and could help escalate the case to the Inspector General's office if needed. Afam made a mental note to call him as soon as he left the police station.

There was a counter at one end of the room, and a long queue had formed, of civilians wishing to visit relatives or friends being held in detention. Behind the counter sat a policeman who was flipping through a thick, hardcover notebook, asking each person, "How can I help you, sir? How can I help you, ma?" There was no computer in the charge room that Afam could see, making him wonder how the station could keep track of their administrative work.

A ceiling fan above his head worked hard to provide some cooling for the room but only ended up making loud screeching noises and circulating hot air. The wall to his right was adorned with portraits of the state governor, the inspector general of police, and the state commissioner of police. The opposite wall seemed to have been turned into a blackboard of some sort, serving as an official portal for registering the number of suspects being held in the station's detention facility. Police uniforms in different states of disorder hung on the walls.

He would not have been here if he wasn't so desperate. The whole atmosphere was depressing. It did not give him any confidence that the police department could help him find his missing niece. It was already three days since she was abducted, and with every new day, his fears that she may have been killed was mounting. If she was to be found, he did not think these policemen would be the ones to do the job. But he had no choice.

After what seemed like an eternity, another policeman came into the charge room and shouted his name. Afam got up and followed him through the crowd into an air-conditioned hallway. They turned into the last door on which a sign read ABU KWAKU, DIVISIONAL POLICE OFFICER. A policeman with a fierce-looking German shepherd stood guard in front of the office.

The chief waved him into a seat and asked, "Did you bring the photographs?"

"Yes, sir."

"Good." He took a sip from a coffee cup and ruffled through a file on his desk. "We got a lead this morning."

Afam nodded.

"The student? Did she really see anything?"

They had spoken on the phone this morning about the young girl from the school who had come forward to say she had seen Kamdi get into the abductor's car during recess that Friday afternoon.

"Oh yes, she did. That Cecilia is a very smart little girl, only eight years old, but she's as sharp as a needle. She remembered the vehicle number, the color of the vehicle. She even told us the car type and model."

Afam's heartbeat quickened. "And?"

"I think she's right. But now we have another problem."

Afam waited for him to continue.

"The owner of the car is well known to us."

"Um…sir, how is that a problem? Aren't you going to question him?"

"Unfortunately, no. It's too risky."

"What—"

"That car belongs to a man we suspect to be one of the leaders of the organized crime mafia in Port Harcourt. They are a band of armed robbers and assassins. They work for many politicians, so they are virtually untouchables. We suspect that they are the gang that recently abducted and killed three people and harvested their kidneys for some high-class clients. It was all over the news. I'm sure you heard about it."

Afam's heart sank. "But what…what are you saying?"

"I know it's hard for you to accept this, but by now, your niece is likely dead—whether in the hands of the kidnappers or of those that sent them. If I was confident that she is still alive, we could try to get involved. But why risk the lives of my officers on a hopeless venture?"

Afam sucked in a deep breath, anger and shock warring in his heart. He stretched out his hands toward the inspector.

"But aren't you even going to try? She might still be alive. There's no body yet."

Mr. Kwaku grabbed his coffee and got up from his chair. He avoided looking in Afam's direction as he walked to the window and drew the curtains aside. Afam watched in frustration as he slowly drank the remainder of the coffee and placed the cup on the windowsill.

"*Oga*, please, sir, you have to do something. I beg you. What if it was your own child that was missing? Wouldn't you put up a fight? Wouldn't you want to bring her abductors to justice? To take them off the streets and ensure that they don't kidnap any more children?"

Mr. Kwaku addressed Afam's question as he walked back to his desk. "We certainly can try if you would like us to. But you will bear the financial cost of the operation yourself. You see, Mr. Izuwa, all the stories you have heard about the police force are true. We have guns but no bullets, we have police cars but no petrol, and we have officers that have not been paid for months. If you can sponsor this operation, we can go after them. Even if she is dead, we can find out what happened to her, and maybe, just maybe, we can arrest some people."

Afam felt as if someone had put a dagger deep into his heart. He felt dizzy and closed his eyes for balance. Countless stories about the ineptitude of the state police he had heard over the years had never bothered him because he'd never had a police case. Now he was experiencing it firsthand. *Police is your friend* indeed. These people were not prepared to inconvenience themselves to answer the call for citizen protection that was supposed to be their occupation. How could he go back to his nephews to tell them there was nothing anybody could do to locate their sister? They were still praying, hoping to see Kamdi home soon. How could he shatter their dreams?

"Look," Mr. Kwaku regarded him over horn-rimmed spectacles, "I anticipated that you would want us to launch a rescue operation. I also anticipated that you would be open to paying for it. Before you came, I drew up a budget for the six operatives I would need to work on the case. This is it." He handed over a piece of paper on which he had handwritten some figures. The writing was difficult to decipher, but Afam's eyes went to the bottom line, and his eyes rose at the millions of naira shown as the total sum.

"You can call me later with your decision. In the meantime, show me the pictures you brought. I hope they are clearer than the ones I took from the house that night. The woman we have in detention could not identify your girlfriend from the pictures I showed her."

Afam opened his briefcase and took out the envelope with pictures of Vickie that he had brought with him. He handed this over to Mr. Kwaku. After examining the photographs, Mr. Kwaku nodded to him and shouted for an officer. When the man appeared, the DPO directed him to come with them to the detention facility for an interview with Ifeoma Nwokorie. Afam managed to control himself and followed them.

They came out of the police station and headed to an adjoining compound that was fenced around with barbed wires and a steel gate. The building they entered had only one door that he could see, and its high-level windows were covered with metal bars. As they passed through the gate, Afam silently wondered if this was a real jail or simply the detention center.

They were led to an interview room situated right at the entrance of the building where a rather large policewoman was waiting with another woman in blue prison uniform. Afam had met Ifeoma on the day he took the children for the Montessori admission tests, but the woman sitting on the lone chair in the room looked nothing like what he remembered of the school receptionist. Bruises on her cheeks, streaks of blood running down from her head, bloodied matted hair, swollen lips, and black eyes were all indicative of how she had been thoroughly roughed up by the police officers since her arrest. He tried not to feel sorry for her, focusing instead on the police chief's theory that she must have been in cahoots with his niece's abductors.

As soon as they arrived, the police chief scattered the photographs of Vickie on the table and asked Ifeoma if she could recognize her as the woman who came to pick up Kamdi from the school. Afam watched her face intently as she slowly looked from one picture to the next. Finally, she looked up and shook her head from side to side.

"No, sir," her voice was hoarse. "She's not the one. She resembles her, but she is not the one. Maybe she has added a lot of weight since she took the picture. Or maybe these pictures were taken a long time ago. But I just don't recognize her here."

Mr. Kwaku looked up questioningly at Afam.

"They are current photos, sir, all taken within the last six months. I downloaded them from my cell phone."

"The woman that came for the children was plump and dark in complexion. I will recognize that woman if I see her again."

"Are you sure?"

"Yes, sir," she confirmed. "Since I came here, three nights now, all I have been doing is thinking about that woman, trying to remember. She had open teeth and a black mark on her face, near one eye. I even thought that she was wearing the sunshade to hide the mark. I didn't know she was trying to disguise herself."

Mr. Kwaku and the policewoman continued to shove photograph after photograph in Ifeoma's face, asking her to take another look, but Afam tuned out after a few minutes to consider her description of the woman who had come for Kamdi at the school. Vickie could never be described as plump, so that would take her right out of the equation. His mind quickly ran through the few ladies in his acquaintance, but none of them fit the description. He remembered something the DPO had said last Friday night, a *man's enemies are usually members of his own family.* Ebele was dark-complexioned and slightly plump, but of course, it could not be her. She was his sister. Plus, she had no gaps in her front teeth. There had to be somebody he knew who reminded him of Ebele.

Then an idea hit him.

"I have other photographs on my cell phone that I can show her, photos of my friends and relations. I have had the same cell phone for over three years. If the woman who showed up to pick up Kamdi from school is someone I know, I may have a photo of her in my gallery."

When the DPO nodded his permission, he leaned closer to Ms. Ifeoma and showed her how to operate the photo gallery. With one hand on her head, she wiped her tears, sucked in a sniffle, and started to flip through the pictures.

Afam and Mr. Kwaku watched her.

She took her time, staring intently at every screen before moving to the next. It was more than two minutes before she pointed at the screen and asked, "Is there another picture of this woman?"

Afam looked at the woman she was pointing to, nodded, and exhaled loudly. He should have known. Without a word, he took the phone from Ifeoma and began to flip through to find another photo of Vickie's sister. There was another picture he had taken of the sisters at a family event he had accompanied her to over a year ago, soon after they met.

"That is the woman who came to pick up the children from school," Ifeoma Nwokorie's voice was strong in her conviction.

"Are you sure?" Mr. Kwaku asked.

"Yes, sir. She's the one. Is that not what I told you? She's black and plump. Can't you see the mark on her face? She is smiling in this picture, and you can see the open teeth. See the resemblance to the other woman in the first picture. But their complexion is very different o! Maybe the other woman bleached her face to become fair. Are they sisters?"

Afam stared grimly at her.

"Thank you," he said and turned off the cell phone.

Ifeoma's eyes began to fill up with tears as she reached out to hold Afam's shirt. "Please, sir, tell them to release me. I had nothing to do with this. I was only doing my work in the school. Since Friday, they have been beating me as if I am a criminal. I am not. I am a Christian woman. Please. I have three children at home. Please, sir, for my children's sake, tell them to let me go. I beg you in Jesus's name. Please, sir. Please…"

Afam felt sorry for her.

"Hey you! Stop that!" the policewoman shouted, slapping the woman's hand from his shirt. "You are not going anywhere until they arrest that woman. How are we sure you are telling the truth?"

The DPO turned to him. Afam nodded.

"Let her go," the police chief directed the policewoman.

"But if I find that you are lying," he warned Ifeoma, "you will be back here before you know what hit you. And if I see you here again, there will be no mercy."

"Never! I know what I am saying, sir. I know who I saw. I am not lying. Thank you, *Oga* DPO. Thank you, *Oga* Izuwa. May God reward your kindness and help you find your niece o! May God answer your prayers o! I will fast and pray for her. You will find her in Jesus's name. God bless you, sir. God…"

It was with grim determination that Afam blocked off her shouts of gratitude and followed Mr. Kwaku out of the detention facility.

CHAPTER 25

The rabbit does not run in the
daytime for nothing.

—African proverb

Awele sat on her sofa with a thick paperback and asked herself for the thousandth time what she was doing. The answer remained the same—she had absolutely no clue. But not knowing what she was doing, or what she was looking for, had not stopped her from mounting a watch over Edem's apartment. There was only one entrance into the bungalow, and it was directly opposite her flat, albeit several yards away. She wanted to see everyone who was going in or coming out from the house and to figure out what they had to do with the imminent sacrifice she had unwittingly learned about four nights ago.

Luckily for her, she was still off sick, having been ordered by the doctor to stay away from work for the rest of the week so she could fully recover from what had been finally diagnosed as typhoid fever. So she stayed put at home and kept watch, waiting for something she didn't know to happen.

She had no idea what it would look like, what shape it would take, or how she would recognize it when it happened. All she knew was that whatever it was would involve Edem. Maybe he would be required to wash the sacrificial animal by himself or rub it with white *nzu* chalk while reciting incantations. Maybe he would be told to bless the animal. Or to beg the animal to take away his sickness. She was not sure. But with so much idle time on her hands, her imagination was working overtime configuring different possibilities.

From her calculations, Pa Edem had only three more days to comply with Chibala's demand, but so far, in the yard, it was business as usual. At least as far as she could see.

Unless it had happened already, and she had not noticed.

How could that be possible? she mused. Of course, it could have happened while she was asleep, or while she was in the washroom taking a shower, or in the kitchen cooking. She hoped she was wrong, that it had not happened yet. It would be too bad if they chose the moment her back was turned to lead an animal into Edem's quarters.

She had stopped herself just in time from telling Tokumbo about the conversation she had overheard the night she was ill. And she had not confided in Dr. Ben for similar reasons—they would have told her to get out of Pa Edem's compound fast.

She had never witnessed animal sacrifices before, and, with any luck, it would not happen in the compound. Wasn't that what Pa Edem had told his friend? That the animal would first be brought to Edem for some ritual and then be slaughtered at the witch doctor's shrine.

The devil is wicked, she thought sadly, as she slowly turned up the volume dial on her radio to listen to the afternoon news. *See how he has blinded the eyes of men and convinced them that slaughtering a goat or sheep can heal a human illness. The poor animals!*

Four days of watching Edem's flat closely had made her see things she had not noticed previously. The house paint had once been an olive green but had worn until it was now mostly gray. The windowsills were also weathered. An old rocker had been placed by the door, and she hoped that one day Edem would sit out there again and play boardgames with his friends in the cool of the evening breeze.

There was movement across the courtyard from her land-lady's quarters. She saw Pa Edem and his wife come out from Ma Edem's bungalow. The landlady was dressed in her double wrapper and white blouse, obviously going somewhere import-ant. After a brief chat, her husband left and walked briskly to the main house while Ma Edem strolled over to Edem's bunga-low. But she didn't stay long in there, just two or three minutes and she was out again then called for the driver to come so they could leave.

Awele glanced at her phone. It was already after ten. Where was Ma Edem off to? Before she could talk herself out of it, she gathered some clothes in her laundry basket and carried them out to hang in the backyard, close to where Ma Edem stood waiting by the car.

"Good morning, madam," she greeted. "I thought you'd already gone to the market."

"Awele!" her landlady sounded shocked. "Are you still sick? Ah, you've lost weight o!"

"I'm getting better every day, ma. The doctor gave me some time off, but I will soon go back to work."

"I see. Please take care of yourself o! Person life no get duplicate."

"I will. Madam, I hope you don't mind my asking, how is Edem doing?

Her landlady hissed and turned her eyes to the ground. "He's as well as can be expected. He is actually talking more now, even eating more."

"Oh, praise God," Awele enthused. "I'm still praying for him. All things are possible."

"Thank you."

"Did he tell you I texted him? Did he read my message?"

"No. I don't believe he told me."

"I sent him a few words to encourage him, to let him know that more people than he realizes are standing with him in this tough time. I sent a prayer request for him and people are praying. I didn't identify him by name, or reveal the nature of the sickness. I just asked for healing prayers."

"It's good of you, Awele. I'm sure he will be happy to know that. But please be careful not to send any preachy messages to him. His father won't be happy if he sees them."

"No problem, madam. I won't. I'm so glad to hear he's getting better. By God's grace, he will continue to get better until the sickness is completely controlled."

The woman looked at her for a few seconds, and Awele perceived she was contemplating telling her something.

"How was Pa Edem's visit with Chibala?" she preempted in a whisper.

"No, Awele, don't ask me. I shouldn't be telling you anything. I cannot tell you anything."

The driver ran up then and started the car. The ladies turned to see Pa Edem walking toward them, and Ma Edem lifted a hand to her mouth to cover a sudden yawn. Then she continued in a louder than normal voice.

"I am going to Ikorafa Secondary School to pick up my husband's niece. She's in the boarding house there. She has fallen ill, and her parents live up north. They want us to take her from the school and nurse her back to health. I'll see you when I get home. Take care of yourself o! This one everyone is falling sick with typhoid and malaria, I wonder what is happening!"

Awele watched her get in the back seat, waving when the driver slowly drove through the gate. When she turned, Pa Edem was squinting at her. She dipped her knees slightly in a brief curtsy.

"Good morning, sir."

"You did not go to work today?"

"No, sir, I've been ill."

"My wife told me you were hospitalized."

Awele wondered if there was a question at the end of that sentence and chose to ignore it. "I'm much better now, sir. I hope to get back to work soon."

"Good," he said and walked off. Awele quickly hung her clothes on the line and hurried back to her room.

She took a brief nap, waking up at quarter past eleven. She went to the bathroom, washed her face in cold water, and scowled at her reflection in the full-length mirror. Her neck was long enough, dehydration from typhoid made it look even longer, enhancing what she described as her peacock look. Her eyes were wider than ever, and her dress hung over her like a drape. She ran a finger along the wide black band that edged the neckline of her dress and tugged at the bodice. Her mother would be shocked if she could see how thin she'd become in just one week. Thinking of her mother, she picked up her phone and dialed her home phone. Her father answered.

"Awele, my dear, how are you? Are you fully recovered from your sickness?" he asked.

"Yes, sir. I'm fine. How is everyone?"

"They are okay. Do you want to talk to your mother?"

Surprised at his abrupt dismissal, she started to say something but he cut her off.

"Here she is," he said and handed the phone to her mother.

"What is the matter with Dad?" she cried to her mother when she came on the line. "You'd think he doesn't know who I am?"

"Don't be angry, my dear. It's just that we are all in a state of emergency here."

"Why? What happened? Did anyone die?" she held her breath for the answer. Any time she was not at home, she always dreaded the day someone would call her to say one of her friends or relatives had passed away. "Is it Grandma?"

"God forbid! Your grandma is fine."

"What then? Who is it?"

"It's the Izuwas! They are in big trouble."

Izuwa? The name sounded familiar. "You mean, Dad's former business partner, the one that died some years ago?"

"Yes, him. His granddaughter was kidnapped last weekend."

"Oh no!"

"She's only eight years old. She was abducted from school on Friday. There's been no ransom notes, no communication from the kidnappers. Everybody is suspecting that she has been kidnapped for ritual purposes."

Awele's eyes widened.

"Oh no!"

"The poor girl and her two brothers recently lost their parents. Afam has been looking after them for just over a month. I told you he is very kindhearted. He just enrolled them in a school and within their first week there, the little girl was kidnapped."

It took a while, but Awele eventually got the whole story out of her mother. She thought about Afam Izuwa, taking on his sister's children and having to deal with such tragedy. It made sense to her that the child could have been kidnapped for sacrifice. Albinos usually were. Awele's father was beside himself with the need to help his late friend's family. If the kidnappers asked for money in exchange for the missing girl, Awele was sure her father would pay up without question.

"Your father has paid for spots on NTA and RSTV and in all the major radio stations. Starting from today and for the next seven days, the search for the child will be on most media outlets. NTA will relay the news every three hours throughout the week, unless we get confirmation that she is no longer alive."

"Poor child. Poor Mr. Izuwa. I will pray for them," she offered. What else could she do? In Nigeria, in times of trial, government forces were not often helpful. Everybody prayed.

"Awele, this is the same Afam Izuwa that I wrote to you about last month. You did receive my letter, didn't you?"

"Yes, I did. Gosh, Mom, this is not the time to discuss that."

"I know. I just wanted to let you know that he's still very interested in meeting you. Phidelia told me that if it wasn't for this crisis, he would have come to visit you in Ituandem before the end of your service year."

After she dropped the phone, Awele went to her table and withdrew the picture of Afam Izuwa that her mother had sent to her. She studied him closely this time, noting the athletic build, the bright eyes, and the gentle smile. His looks were a mix of class, sophistication, and success. *He had to be a kind man*, she thought, *this young man that had embraced his sister's children as his own.* He must also be a man of integrity, judging from her own father's commitment to helping him. There had to be something special about him to make her mother earmark him for a son-in-law. Her lips broke into a rueful smile as she looked at the picture again. He did look nice but it would probably never happen between them. It irritated her that a grown-up man would let his mother arrange a marriage for him.

She turned on her television to try and catch the announcement on the NTA *News at Noon*. Sure enough, there was the picture of the serious-looking albino girl who had been kidnapped at the weekend. While the announcer rattled off contact phone numbers for people to report sightings of the child, Awele tried to memorize her face. Afterward, she knelt by her bed and prayed that the missing girl would be found and that Afam Izuwa's mind would be at peace.

At noon, Awele heard her landlord's voice and looked through her windows. He was with the *mai-guard* at the gate, directing a truck bearing wooden planks into the compound. If he was at the gate that meant Edem would be alone in his room. Before thinking it through, she picked up her phone. "Hi," she texted, "Heard you are getting better. So happy. Praying. Complete healing. Cheers!"

Awele watched as the driver and his mate worked together to remove the plank sheets from the truck. Later, they followed Pa Edem around as he pointed out some parts of the courtyard to them. She wondered what they could be up to as she went to the fridge to bring out ingredients for the vegetable soup she would cook for dinner. She took the cutting board to her small dining table and began to chop *ugu* vegetables into tiny pieces. Awele kept her window open and watched as the men brought out shovels and began to dig up the ground at different points in the compound. Then they started to knock wooden panels together. It wasn't too long before she realized they were erecting a fence between her flat and the rest of the compound.

Awele knew an uneasy feeling then that the day of the sacrificial offering had finally come.

CHAPTER 26

When will the goat be strong
enough to kill a leopard?

—African proverb

"Why did the DPO send for you today?"

Afam looked up from his dinner. It was a quiet evening. Too quiet. These days, his house was so quiet you could hear a pin drop. He sat at the dinner table every evening only because his mother was watching over him like a hawk. She would not let him get away with missing his meals. Still, between the two of them, dinner had become a silent affair.

"He said someone called with news that they saw a child that looked like Kamdi last Saturday night."

Startled, Phidelia didn't know when her spoon dropped to her plate, scattering the fried rice on the table. "Are you serious?

"Yes. The person said the child was in the trunk of a Peugeot 505, not the SUV that Cecilia had identified."

Phidelia's hands went to her chest, and her heartbeat picked up a faster rhythm. "In the trunk of a car? Oh my God, was she—"

Afam shook his head. "I don't know."

"But still, this is a good lead, no? There is still hope that she can be found. Why are you looking so sad? Let me guess—they are not going to investigate it?"

Afam nodded and sighed. "Unfortunately, no."

Horrified, Phidelia could only stare at him.

"First of all, the caller was anonymous. Since Chief Martins put out the reward money for any lead on Kamdi's whereabouts, there have been lots of bogus calls."

"But for him to call you about this one, he must think it is true."

"He does," Afam agreed. "The caller even provided him with the names of the two men who drove the car. He was able to successfully confirm one of them as the driver of the car used to kidnap Kamdi from school."

He paused, shaking his head. "The problem is that they are notorious, heavily armed assassins. Mr. Kwaku is not willing to risk the life of his men against criminals with greater mortar power than his entire police force."

"Ah! God!' Phidelia buried her face in her hands. "What is this country turning into? Have we become so corrupt? Have we lost all decency and moral standards? Evil is running rampant on our streets. Innocent people are being killed. Criminals are roaming about in broad daylight. The police are afraid of them. Oh my god!"

Afam reached for his water but held on to the glass, staring ahead with unseeing eyes, lost in contemplation. It was his mother's voice that broke into his brooding.

"There's more, isn't there?" She knew him only too well. "My son, what else did Mr. Kwaku tell you? Why is your heart so heavy?"

He stared at his mother vacantly for a few seconds. "The tipster said the child he saw in the car looked—" His voice broke and he shook his head. He dropped his head into his hands, and Phidelia watched the tears escape from his hands as he sobbed quietly. "The tipster said the child he saw looked... dead."

"No!" she screamed. "No! No! No!" she screamed again, so loudly that the servants ran in to find out what was happening. Phidelia's tears were flowing, and she was rocking back and forth in emotional pain. Afam looked up and motioned to Amadi and his wife to leave them alone. He did not want to talk about this to anyone yet.

"*Nne*, listen. I didn't believe him. I don't believe she's the one the caller saw. I think Mr. Kwaku is just looking for an excuse to call off the investigations."

Phidelia dug up a white handkerchief from the folds of her outer wrapper, dabbed at her eyes, and blew her nose.

"Chief Martins agrees with me."

"He does?"

"Yes. I called him as soon as I left the police station. He said juju priests do not accept dead animals or dead humans for sacrifice. If indeed the abductors want her for ritual, she wouldn't be dead. It's possible that the caller was confused about what he saw. He said it all happened very quickly, and that it was at night. So he didn't even get the vehicle's license plate number, but he clearly remembered the names of the two men in the vehicle."

Phidelia nodded as she thought over his words. "Chief Martins is probably right. I hope he's right. I hope you are both right and she's not dead, if only for the sake of those two boys in that room. They are very convinced that she will be saved."

Mother and son were silent for a long time, only Phidelia's sniffles could be heard. Afam was physically tired and mentally exhausted. He could not believe that with all the evidence they had gathered so far—from the child Cecilia, from the school receptionist, and now from the anonymous caller—the police could not even pretend to be searching for Kamdi. Even if she was dead like the DPO claimed, wouldn't they look for her body, or at least question the people already identified by eyewitnesses? Even Rachel, Vickie's sister, had not been interviewed. Mr. Kwaku said he needed more information before he could question her.

"Hogwash!" he muttered under his breath. "Complete rubbish. He's still asking me to pay for their so-called search and rescue operation. If I was convinced that they would go after those kidnappers, of course I will pay. But they just want money. They would just divide the cash among themselves, and after three days, they will either ask for more money or spin me a tale of how they 'almost' caught the kidnappers. This country is sick," he concluded in disgust.

"I agree, and those policemen know exactly what they are doing. If they wanted to find that poor child, I bet you they would have. They know the kidnappers, but to them, she's not worth their efforts. She's an albino, a poor child with no connections to any politician, an obvious prey for the witch doctors whom the politicians consult for power. To them, she's expendable, easy to forget. They believe her death won't mean anything to anybody."

Afam shook his head slowly from side to side, trying in vain to rein in the grief that consumed his heart. When it burst out, he banged his hands on the table and let out a suppressed groan.

"Why are human beings so wicked, Mama?" he spoke through clenched teeth. "Why do we take delight in considering others inferior to ourselves because of the color of their skin? We're all the same—black, white, and all the shades between. We have no control over our genes. Kamdi is one of us, created equally, on the same earth, under the same sun, under the same moon. And no, she's not easy to forget. I won't forget her.

Neither will you. Nor will those two boys who have not ceased to pray day and night for her safe return."

He wished there was something he could do to move the investigation along. But the police were not interested in helping him. He had asked for the name of the anonymous tipster, so he could contact him, but the DPO had replied that the caller was anonymous for a reason. Nor would Kwaku give him the names of the kidnappers the caller had provided him.

Peter and John were waiting for him to bring their sister home. How could he explain to them that in Nigeria, you are held ransom by the very system that is supposed to protect you? Or that if he wanted any progress in the search for Kamdi, he had to first cough up millions of naira to the police force and then wait, in hope that they will follow through on their commitment, knowing that there is no recourse if they don't.

Just then, he heard the quiet voices of his young nephews interrupt the evening silence. They were singing a simple song that had become achingly familiar to him.

"I have a God who never fails, who never fails, who never fails, forevermore!"

Their songs and prayers had become an accepted part of the household routine. Every few hours, everyone would hear them singing. Or praying. Or both. The adults marveled that two young boys going through such unimaginable suffering could sing so confidently, so trustingly of an unseen God. Everyone pitied them. They were just children, living in a fantasy world and didn't know any better. Yet no one dared discourage them.

Afam heard a moan and turned to his mother. She was sniffing, wiping tears from her eyes. He watched her for a few minutes, saw the sniffle turn to hiccups and more tears. He got up from his seat and went to her. Gently, he led her to the sofa, sat beside her, and folded her in his arms. The sobbing continued as they held on to each other.

"I can't help it," she sobbed. "That poor child. These poor boys. I cannot bear it! I can't."

Afam murmured words of comfort from a heavy heart. "We'll get through this, Mama. Let's just stay strong."

"Oh God," he heard her pray. "Please hear the prayers of these children. Oh God, please do a miracle and bring the girl home. *Biko nu Chineke*, please bring Kamdi home."

Afam held her until her sobbing subsided. Finally, when she was spent and he looked down, he was not sure if it was his or her tears that had dampened his shirt.

She reached for the Kleenex box on the side table and blew her nose. "When is their aunt's flight arriving?"

He checked his smartphone. "In less than two hours. According to my tracker, their plane has just landed in Lagos and should be taking off for Port Harcourt soon."

"Good. Take the boys to the airport when you pick her up. Let this be a surprise to them, something to cheer them up."

Afam intended to do exactly that. It had been his mother's suggestion to send for Binta Garuba. Their aunt was a familiar face. She had been with the children through the loss of their parents, and she could reach them in a way nobody in his household could.

Afam had never appreciated his mother as he had this past week. He couldn't imagine how he could have gone through this crisis without her support. He couldn't even remember why he had been so anxious for her to leave his home in the first place. Now he was glad she hadn't listened to him.

He got up to put on the television for the evening news. The spot announcement about Kamdi came after the first commercial break. Afam was thankful to Chief Martins for the publicity. His father's former partner had been extremely helpful throughout this ordeal. Afam had relayed to him all the information he had heard from DPO Kwaku, and he was already making the case with the police Inspector-General for a federal intervention. Mother and son watched as Kamdi's face filled the screen and slowly faded out.

Five minutes later, his phone rang, and he looked at the caller ID. It was Vickie. He contemplated for a moment before he hit the green button.

"Hello, Vickie!" he said quietly.

"Oh, Afam," her voice came through the line, loud and teary. "Afam, I'm so sorry. I just heard the news about your niece. Have they found her? Is she okay?"

From the corner of his eyes, he saw anger replace the sorrow in his mother's eyes. He tried to suppress his own anger. His one regret was that it had taken him over one year and possibly the life of his niece to see his erstwhile girlfriend for who she truly was. But he was not ready to antagonize her yet. He had to find out what she knew about Kamdi's abduction. The DPO had said he could not arrest her unless he had solid evidence that she was part of the abduction plot.

"No, she's not back home. We haven't seen her yet. It's been five days now."

"But have you heard from the kidnappers? What are they asking for?"

"Not a word. We're still waiting."

"And the police? What are they saying?"

"Nothing. Everyone is waiting to hear from the kidnappers. They said they cannot do much until they know what they are fighting against."

"Oh, I'm so sorry, Afam."

"Are you in town?" he asked her.

"No, I'm still in Lagos. I've not been in Port Harcourt since I left early last week. You know I would have come immediately I heard the news if I was still there. How is your mother? Is she still hating me?"

"My mother?" he tried to sound dismissive. "Hmm. I doubt that she still feels that way. We are all focused on finding Kamdi now and desperate for help from any and everyone. I'm reaching out to all my friends and family for any information that might lead to her rescue. So, if there's anything you can do to help, we will be very grateful."

There was silence from the other side of the phone before she asked quietly, a smile in her voice. "Am I still in your circle of friends and family, Afam?"

"Of course."

"Are you sure, Afam?"

"Absolutely. Vickie, I've told you before, we don't have to be married to be friends. I still consider you one of my best friends. I'm still waiting for you to fully explain why you wanted me to get rid of Kamdi the day you met her. Other than that, you are welcome anytime."

There was a pause from her side. His graciousness seemed to have caught her off guard.

"You have to admit that I was right about your niece, though. I know you love her and all that, but see, she's already brought pain into your life. Not on purpose, of course. But there are spiritual forces in this world against albinos, and it is best if they are kept away from real human beings."

Afam could not believe his ears. "Vickie, are you saying albinos are not human beings?"

"I didn't say so, but you know that witch doctors have claimed them for the gods since time immemorial. They are not normal people. They cause more problems for their families than they are worth."

"How can you believe that, Vickie? That girl you saw in my house was every bit as human as you and I."

Vickie went silent, perhaps allowing his anger to cool down before sighing.

"Afam Izuwa, you have not changed o! I was hoping this incident will teach you a few things, but you are not learning fast enough. I see I still have more work to do on you."

Afam closed his eyes to contain his emotions. "Not on me, you don't," he whispered silently. "*Why, oh why had he allowed himself to be associated with a woman like this?*" She was evil, pure evil. Why hadn't he seen it before now?

"Are you still there?"

"Mm hmm."

"I have to go now. I will catch the evening flight tomorrow and be there before dinner. If I cannot make it tomorrow evening, I will catch the first flight the next day. Is that okay?"

After he dropped the phone, Afam called Amadi.

"Tell Peter and John I want to see them. They are to change their clothes before they come because I am taking them out. And tell Musa to gather Vickie's paraphernalia into a garbage bag, she's coming either tomorrow or the day after to pick them. He is to give them to her outside the gate. He must not let her into my compound ever again."

CHAPTER 27

If you do not eat yam for the sake of palm oil,
you will eat palm oil for the sake of yam.

—African proverb

Awele listened to laughter from the living room as she searched her fridge in the kitchen for an empty spot to place the vegetable soup.

A delegation from the hospitality team of Grace Side Assembly was in her living room. Her absence from both the Sunday service and Wednesday night Bible study in the past week had not gone unnoticed. As news of her sickness had spread, so also had the number of phone calls and text messages and e-mails from brethren wishing her speedy recovery. And now, they had sent two young adults from the church to bring their well-wishes in person.

She appreciated their thoughtfulness and the visit, but how in the world did they expect her to eat all the food they had brought? At this rate, she would have to offer some to Dr. Ben to give to his patients.

Before going back to the living room, she decided to cut oranges to serve them. Luckily, she had banana and groundnuts to add, and some fruit juice. She brought out the oranges and washed them in the sink. She had just peeled the rind off one when she heard a light tapping on the kitchen door. Drying her hands, Awele strolled to the door and pulled it open.

Tokumbo and Dr. Ben Adakole stood on the welcome mat. She could see from the two grocery bags Ben was carrying that they had brought more food for her.

She groaned inwardly but plastered a smile on her face. Where was she going to store all this food?

"Hi, Toks. Hi, Dr. Ben. Did you walk down here? I didn't hear your car drive in?"

"Haven't you looked outside your window lately? There's nowhere to park. What's with the barricade?"

Awele shrugged. "I don't have a single clue what my landlord is up to. The walls went up this afternoon. I don't want to complain because, as you can see, he did leave a path for my car to pass through and somewhere for me to park it. The gateman told me that his *oga* has directed that all visitors must park outside the compound for the time being. Even his own visitors must park outside, so who am I to complain?"

They heard voices from her living room, and Dr. Ben took a step forward to see who was visiting. "I see you have company. Is this a good time? We only wanted to see how you were doing."

"Of course, come in. They are from church. You will recognize Brother Simon and Sister Theresa. Go in and visit with them while I arrange the fruits to serve them. I'm almost done."

Her two friends looked at each other, then Tokumbo shook her head. "No worries, we won't intrude. Give me a call, and we will come back when they are gone. We have something to tell you."

Awele looked at her friend intently. From the shy smile playing on her lips and the sly glance at Dr. Ben, she did not want to wait for long if the direction of her thoughts could be confirmed now.

"Tell me now, please!" she insisted.

Dr. Ben had the grace to look embarrassed but the big smile across Tokumbo's face said it all.

"Emm...you two?" she whispered in excitement.

Tokumbo nodded in affirmation.

"For real...?"

Tokumbo nodded again.

"Oh, my goodness, Toks!... I can't believe this. Are you serious?"

"Of course!" her friend's happiness shone through.

Awele reached out and hugged her tight. "Oh my god! Congratulations! This is the best news ever! I always thought the two of you should get together. I didn't know you were also thinking the same. This is so crazy. So exciting. So good!"

"You don't mind, Awele, do you?"

"Mind?" she screeched excitedly. "Me? You've got to be joking. You guys are my two best friends in the world right now. I couldn't be happier. But you're right. Let me attend to my visitors for an hour or two. Then you must come back and tell me all about it. I'm *soooo* excited for you two."

They dropped the grocery bags and left, and Awele returned to the oranges in the sink. She smiled as she peeled off the rinds with a paring knife, rejoicing for her friends. She'd known that Tokumbo liked Dr. Ben even though the doctor had been concentrating all his attention on her for almost a year now. Tokumbo had even admitted as much to her. She wondered what her friend had done to finally get him to notice her. Whatever it was, she was glad it had worked. Tokumbo was mature and ready for marriage and would make a good doctor's wife.

When she joined them in the living room, her visitors were swapping internet jokes. Awele smiled, and listened attentively so she could catch on. This was the internet generation, with its abundance of knowledge and easy access through any smartphone. Combined with Nigerians' love for fun and laughter and for making fun of themselves, the internet had become a ready tool for a good time.

"As you know," she heard Simon say, "Nigerians are experts at everything, both good and bad. Oyibo people say we are over-achievers. When it comes to making money, we're there. When it comes to committing crime, we're there. When it comes to great acts of kindness, we're also there. Our economy has no cure. Our politics is corrupt. Our schools and hospitals are broken. Yet we seem to be thriving, by hook and mostly by crook, to the consternation of everyone."

"It's true o, my brother," Sister Theresa agreed. "How many times have I heard it said that the country will soon collapse, but here we are…many decades later, still standing… or, to be more accurate, still wobbling."

"No leave, no transfer."

They laughed. Awele smiled and set the fruits before them.

"I read a story on the internet recently." Awele's excitement for Dr. Ben and Tokumbo was making her talkative. "It's actually a joke, but the moral is that Nigerians cause trouble everywhere they go, even in the afterlife."

"Tell us," her visitors pleaded.

"So," she began, her voice brimming with laughter, "apparently, there was a crisis in hell, which caused the devil to call God and ask him to come and remove all the Nigerians from hell."

"What?"

"The devil was complaining to the Lord that the Nigerians in hell were causing too much havoc for him and his demons and that he couldn't control them. The Nigerians had installed air conditioners everywhere, beat up the demons, and chased them away, so much so that the demons went on strike, saying they won't go back to work until the Nigerians were removed from there."

By now, everyone was laughing. Awele was holding her sides with the pain of deep laughter.

"And what did the Lord tell him?"

"God told him to sort it out, that after all he was the one who deceived the Nigerians not to worship him. So now he, that is, the devil, had to deal with them. Needless to say, the devil was totally frustrated."

From swapping jokes, the visitors turned to politics and public affairs, and soon they were all listening to the evening news on television with rapt attention. Awele left them to rinse and cut the big pawpaw that Ben and Tokumbo had brought for her and added the slices to the fruit tray. When she took her seat by her small dining table, she saw why the news was so captivating. It was about the missing albino girl on the gossip TV station, Word-On-The-Street television channel. She listened. The newscaster was saying:

WOTS has received confirmed reports that the car has been sighted in Ikorafa. A listener contacted News Express to say that on Saturday night, the day after the girl was declared missing, he accidentally opened the trunk of a car in Ikorafa and saw the body of an albino girl wrapped in a garri sack. He said he called the police and reported, but up until now, no arrests have been made, and the child is still missing. The police have released a statement warning the public that the kidnappers are to be considered armed and dangerous. If you see the car, or the child, do not approach them. Instead, call your nearest police station on 1-080-POLICE.

The news continued with a panel discussion on the recent wave of abductions raising fear across the country. The panelists talked about increase in political and terrorist kidnappings and concluded that most abductions were driven largely by economic hardships. When Awele passed the fruit tray around again, she succeeded in bringing her visitors' attention back to the living room. But their conversation only picked up from where the TV news had stopped.

"In my village, we have at least two albinos," Sister Theresa remarked. "They don't go out. They are always indoors come rain or shine. How terrible to be living with this type of fear."

"That is the worst kind. Not being able to trust even your neighbor."

"You're talking of neighbor. I should think that if you were an albino you would be afraid of even your own brothers and sisters."

"That is so true. This man that this girl was living with, how are you sure his hands are clean in this matter? They say he is young and rich. How did he make his money? Young people of nowadays will do anything to get rich quick. I won't put it past him to have planned the whole thing with the witch doctors. First, they pretend to kidnap her. Then they kill and dismember her body, use her body parts for their rituals, and later turn around to tell everyone they never found her. That's what they do."

"No, please don't say that," Awele interrupted. "Let us not rush to conclusions. Let's not judge someone we don't even know."

"Sister Awele, please be realistic," Brother Simon responded. "This is Nigeria. We're living in a jungle. Survival of the fittest is the rule here. People just do whatever they think they can get away with."

"After listening to this news, all I can think about now is that Ikorafa is only fifty kilometers from Ituandem," Sister Theresa admitted. "I'm thinking we should all be vigilant in case the kidnapper comes this way. We have to be prepared to call the police if we see anything suspicious."

As the discussion was going on, Awele heard the sound of the landlord's car from the gate. Ma Edem would be back.

She went to her window to look and saw for the first time how effectively the barricade had obstructed her view of the compound. She stretched her neck, focusing through the gaps between the planks. Luckily, there was a small gap right at her eye level, wide enough for her to barely see the landlady's front door.

She heard Ma Edem's voice talking to the gateman. "Na wetin dey happen?" she asked him. "Who put up this barricade here?"

"Na *oga,* ma," the gateman replied.

"Ah-ah! Why *na*?"

Awele listened as the woman stepped out of the car and shut the door. There was a fainter sound, which she knew was the opening and closing of another car door. She saw Ginika emerge, carrying a child across her shoulder. The sick niece she had gone to pick from school, Awele assumed. The child was completely covered with a wrapper so Awele could not see her face. As Ma Edem questioned the gateman about the reason for the new fence, Ginika and the child disappeared into the house.

"Oh, look at the time," she heard Brother Simon exclaim and turned from the window. "Sister Awele, we should really be on our way. Hopefully, we have cheered you up a bit. Let's have a word of prayer before we head out."

CHAPTER 28

*When a man gets into trou-
ble, he remembers his god.*

—African proverb

"Thank you for bringing me home to see the children, sir,"
a quiet voice floated up to Afam as he sat in the living
room, watching reruns of the public service announcement
about Kamdi.

He turned to see Binta Garuba looking at him from the
doorway. Her Hausa accent was more pronounced than the
boys'. He took a sip from his water bottle and invited her in.

"You've been able to finally tear yourself away from them."

Since her arrival last night, she had spent every waking
moment with the boys. He had heard them talking until midnight, and early this morning, they had started the day with
singing and praying.

Afam was glad. In his assessment, flying Binta home from
Scotland to see her nephews could be the only good thing he
had ever done for the children. The look on their faces when
they saw her at the airport yesterday was priceless. They had
never been to an airport before and had been too polite to ask
why he was taking them there; so they had been truly surprised.
They had stood looking at their aunt for several seconds, not

quite believing their eyes, before racing to fling themselves into her arms and hugging her tight.

"I told them that I had a few things to discuss with you."

He motioned for her to sit and turned down the TV volume.

"I cannot begin to tell you how sorry I am about everything. I never imagined that this would happen. Otherwise, I would never have let her leave this house or this compound."

"It's not your fault, sir. With children like Kamdi, it's always one thing or the other, so one just must be very careful. Inherent human wickedness always finds a way to express itself. Even I must watch out for myself all the time. Just as Kamdi is too fair in complexion, there are those who think I am too dark, and they look down on me because of it. There is prejudice and discrimination everywhere. You're either too black or too fair, from this tribe or from the other, too rich or too poor. There's no end to it."

Afam could understand that. Binta's complexion was almost totally black, a glaring contrast with the flashing white of her eyes and her teeth.

"You should have given some of your color to Kamdi and taken some of hers." He smiled.

"You're right." She laughed. "Then we would have both been like mulattoes. But those ones have their own issues as well. Some people think they are the children of *Mammywota*, the river goddess. We would still have been fighting for our lives. One of my classmates is from India. She said that over there, they still have discrimination based on their skin tones. And we know there is open racism against black people in the western world. It's everywhere. Human nature is evil."

Afam nodded. "You're right. In every culture, race and skin color differences always breed conflicts. We accept colors in flowers, colors in animals, colors in food and vegetables, but we think colors in human beings is bad."

"Yes," Binta agreed, "we are a lost race without God."

Afam had no response to that. However, now that he had her under his roof again, he had a few questions to ask about Kamdi.

"The children say she's been kidnapped before."

"Oh yes, and it was only the grace of God that rescued her from someone who wanted to use her for rituals. We are now praying for another miracle, asking the Lord to send his angels to watch over her and bring her home safe and sound."

He was not sure about that. Maybe this was a good time to give her the latest updates. "Someone said they saw her dead body."

She exhaled a deep breath. "I heard that on the news last night. I will not believe it until I see it. Until they show me her dead body, I'm just going to keep on believing that she's alive and will come home to us one day. And soon."

Now he knew where the boys got their stubborn faith from. Ogugua and her husband must have held this same faith. It baffled him that anyone could believe so strongly in something they had never seen. With the children, he could understand, but surely, adults, specifically Binta who has experienced her share of tragedies, should know better.

"Is this what you've been telling the boys? You shouldn't be encouraging them, you know. Parents who make their children believe that Father Christmas is the one buying the presents they themselves bought are only setting up the children for future disappointment."

"How do you mean?"

"You shouldn't be telling them to hold on to hope where there is none. We should rather be thinking of a way to let them know that she may never be found alive and teach them how to cope with the loss."

He sensed her immediate withdrawal and almost wished he had not said anything. But he was only telling the truth, and even if the children could not accept it yet, she was old enough to face the facts.

She hesitated a moment before looking up and responding in her quiet voice. "But that would be inconsistent with our faith. The children and I...we believe in God. We believe that he is real and that he answers prayers. We live in hope."

"Even after the cruel murder of their parents?"

"God didn't kill them. Boko Haram did."

"Why didn't he stop it? Why didn't he save them from Boko Haram?"

"Sir, as long as we are in this world that is ruled by human beings, we cannot escape the effects of man's fallen nature. We believe that God can save us, but even if he doesn't, death is not the worst thing that can happen to a believer."

"Really? What can be worse than death?"

"Eternal separation from God is worse than death. That would be like dying two times. We believe that since Sister Ogugua and Brother Dan faithfully served the Lord in this life, they will inherit the promise of eternal life with him, and that if we continue in faith, we will be reunited with them when our time on earth is over."

Afam looked steadily at her, a little irked by the way her words made him feel. The hypocrisy of many people who profess Christianity had convinced him that there were no more sincere Christians today, and that the whole religion thing was fake. But there was no argument he could muster against the faith of his young nephews and the sincerity that rang in this woman's voice. Their eyes held for a few seconds as she waited. He did not want to be preached to, so he changed the subject.

"Why didn't you tell me that Kamdi is not my sister's biological child?"

Binta closed her eyes and took a deep breath.

"Because I didn't want to give you a reason to reject her," she explained, hands spread out, pleading for understanding. "On the day I brought them to you, you were already adamant that you couldn't take them on. When you changed your mind, I knew that telling you she was not your biological niece would complicate things, give you a reason to reject all of them, and I was really desperate for you to accept them. But really, Kamdi is Ogugua's daughter. I do not know of any child more loved by her family than she is loved. I'm sorry that I deceived you."

He looked at her and knew she was telling the truth. The sincerity of her heart was evident in the apology he saw in her eyes.

"You're right. I would not have agreed to take any of them if I had known the truth."

Another silence ensued. Binta looked nervous. She bit down on her lips and waited for him to speak. He did not know what else to say to her, so he turned his attention once more to the television screen. The news analysis had started.

"Thank you for taking care of them, sir," she said when the commercials started. "The boys look good and appear to have adjusted well. They showed me their new clothes and shoes. They came to you with very little, but now they have closets filled with stuff."

Afam nodded. "It's been a pleasure. They are good kids."

He paused, then squinted as he remembered something. "You know, Kamdi has to be the sweetest little girl I have ever known. After you left them that day, she cried and cried like I've never seen any person cry. But the next day, she was so sweet. She apologized and said she would never cry again and begged me not to send them away because of her. I promised her that day that I would look after them. She kept her promise. I've never heard her cry since that day." He shook his head. "It looks like I failed to keep mine."

"You mustn't think so, sir. This is the world we live in, full of darkness and wickedness. There was nothing you did that was wrong. Even when she comes back, she still has to go to school. She cannot live her entire life locked up so she doesn't get kidnapped."

Afam nodded.

"I have posted the abduction on social media," she continued. "I already set up a Facebook account with her photographs and information. Many people I know are tweeting and retweeting the story. It should not be difficult for people to recognize her if they see her. There aren't too many albinos in Nigeria these days."

When Binta left him to visit with Amadi and Nneka in the kitchen, he checked his phone, and there was a text message from the DPO to call him. He stepped into his study and put the call through.

"Have you arrested Rachel Ufobia?" he asked when the officer answered.

"I'm afraid not."

"But why?"

"Orders from above."

"I can't believe this, sir. What do you mean by 'orders from above'? It's been almost a week now since the school receptionist identified her as the one who came to the school to pick up my niece and you still have not arrested her, not even for questioning."

"I don't answer to you, Mr. Izuwa. You're not the one paying my salary. My superiors have taken the decision that the case should go cold, and I have no option but to comply."

Afam was furious all over again! How could public officers get away with being so rude and insufferable, with no care for the job they were employed to do for citizens?

"I hope you and your superiors are ready to face the court of public opinion on this decision," he challenged the police chief. "Believe me when I say that this is not the end of it. I will go to the press. I will go to court. If no effort is made to find and return my niece, I will make sure that all of you—you and your superiors—pay dearly. How can you all just fold your hands and let this child die? Think about it, sir," his voice broke. "What if it were your daughter? Would you just accept these decisions from your superior? Would you?"

His voice was rising with every sentence, anger mixed with frustration. He heard someone open the door to the study and saw his mother step in quietly. "Please, sir, you've got to reconsider."

"Listen to me," the DPO interrupted him sharply. "I am on your side, okay? I am not against you. I do not know what they want, but when orders from the governor's office are sent directly to me, threatening to fire me from my position if I continue searching and investigating your niece's disappearance, I have to think of myself and of my own family. I don't want to die. I don't want my wife to be a widow, or my daughters to become fatherless." He paused, and Afam heard him exhale before continuing in a quiet, measured tone. "Now, listen carefully. I want to tell you something in confidence. I think we were getting too close to the truth with the identification of that woman, but she either has strong connections with the government, or is related to someone with strong ties with the government. Someone leaked information to her that she was under surveillance, and she went straight to the government house, and now we have been ordered to back off."

Afam felt weak. He reached for a chair and sat down. It was either that or fall on the floor.

"Help me, sir. Please advise me. What can I do?"

There was another pause, broken only by Afam's heavy breathing, as he waited for the policeman to respond.

"Your suggestion to create publicity on the case is a good one. It may cost you your goodwill with the governor, and you may never get any contracts from this government, but if you are prepared to pay the price, then go for it. Something else you can do is to appeal to the police headquarters in Abuja. That will cost you money, but if you can convince them to take on the case, they are your best bet for finding your niece, alive or dead. The Federal Mobile Police has authority over the state bureaus, and they are incredibly efficient. This is all I can advise you. I will still keep my eyes and ears open, and if I see or hear anything that may be useful, I will pass it on to you."

The full extent of the hopelessness of the situation washed over Afam as soon as the DPO dropped the phone. Totally drained, he dropped the handset, put his head on his reading table, and inhaled deeply. Tears filled his eyes and slipped through his clenched fingers. His mother came to stand by him, gently massaging his neck and shoulders, patting him.

"Mama, it's too late," he said in a broken whisper. "The police won't look for her. The whole thing is part of an organized crime ring. They know who is responsible but don't want to expose them. They don't care whether she is dead or alive."

Phidelia continued the massage until his sobs subsided.

"I have to call Chief Martins," he told her. "I'll ask him to put pressure on the IG in Abuja. I'm not giving up, Mama. I promised that child that I will look after her, and I won't stop until I find her."

Phidelia pulled a chair close to him and sat down. When she did not say anything, he looked up and found her watching him grimly.

"My son," she finally said, quietly. "I think it's time we really turned to God for help. You cannot carry this load by yourself. It's too much."

"What?" he whispered.

She clasped her hand in his and squeezed tight. "I want us to pray. This is Nigeria, my son. God is our only hope."

CHAPTER 29

Who knows whether you have come
to the kingdom for such a time as
this and for this very occasion?

—Esther 4:14

Awele's conversation with Tokumbo lasted well into the night. She wanted to know everything, from how she had managed to get Dr. Ben's attention to how he finally proposed. Tokumbo explained that the two had gone out a few times in the past, long before Awele came to serve at Ituandem. Back then, he had been too occupied with setting up his private clinic to commit any time to building a relationship with anyone. Then, not long after he was done with the clinic, Awele had come to Ituandem and he had become infatuated with her. But they had started talking again in the past two months, and things had gotten much better between them in the two weeks that Awele had been battling typhoid fever.

"I hope you really don't mind, Awele. I know he thinks he's in love with you, but you've always said you don't have romantic feelings for him, so I didn't think you would mind if I helped him see things differently."

"Of course, I don't mind. I like Dr. Ben. I wish he was my brother, that's all. I am happy for you. Really! It's a good thing my service year is coming to an end soon. When I finally leave Ituandem the two of you will be able to explore your relationship without any interference."

Tokumbo laughed. "You're so right, Awele. I told him you wouldn't mind, but he still thinks you must be disappointed."

"Absolutely not! I am super excited for you both. I could not have wished for a better bride for him. I know you will make him an excellent wife. You love him already, and I'm sure he loves you too. That's the most important thing."

"Who said anything about love? I am committed to making our relationship work, to being a good wife to him, and a good mother to our children. And he has promised me the same. That is enough for now."

Awele hesitated for only a moment before responding. "If that is what you want, Toks, go for it. Love can grow for different couples in a multitude of ways."

"It's not that I don't believe in love," Tokumbo hastened to assure her. "I think that with time and patience, love can develop between two people if they are interested enough to work at it. But, as you've heard me say before, I think romantic love is overrated."

"Yet you have been in love with him secretly for a long time. If you had not been, Toks, you would not have accepted him so readily. I know he's not the first person to ask for your hand in marriage. Why didn't you accept the other proposals if you didn't care for romance?"

As they continued dissecting the details of the new relationship, Awele silently gave thanks to God for this unforeseen solution to a testy situation. If Dr. Ben had continued to insist that he wanted to marry her, their relationship would eventually have been destroyed. Now that his interest was focussed on Tokumbo, the three of them could continue their friendship for many more years.

"Awele, what are you looking for in a man?"

"Toks, I'm tired." She yawned. "Do I have to answer that question now? I thought we were talking about you."

"I still want to know."

Awele thought of the answer, and for a few seconds, she could not answer. "Umm, let's say I will know him when I see him."

"You see my point? It's all a mirage. You don't even know what you want."

"Sure, I do." She closed her eyes, trying to recount. "My man is a good man, friendly, kindhearted, a committed Christian of course, educated, able to provide for me and our children, and he loves me."

Tokumbo burst out laughing. "That's it?"

"Em, yes. That's it. What's so funny?"

Tokumbo continued to laugh. "Awele, can't you see? Dr. Ben is all that, and you rejected him."

Awele thought about that for a second. Tokumbo had a point. "But my heart doesn't skip when I see him," she responded quietly. "My blood doesn't heat up in excitement at the sound of his voice. My hands don't itch to touch him. The thought of making babies with him does not keep me awake at night. I don't long to hold him tight and kiss him hard and never let go. I'm looking for all that and more!"

Tokumbo was not laughing anymore. "Hmm. Awele, you're really living in a dream world. Don't you know that those things exist only in romantic novels? They're not real. One day, you'll wake up from your dream world and realize life's not like that."

"Maybe you're right. But until that day, my friend, I will continue to believe what I believe, which is that I will love the man, and he will love me, too, before I marry him."

Their conversation continued until Awele's loud yawns signaled that she had had enough. "Person body no be firewood," she finally said. "I've had a busy day and my body needs some rest. Good night, Toks. You and Ben owe me lunch one of these days o! We must celebrate o!"

She got up to turn off her lights and connect her cell phone to the charger. As soon as her head hit the pillow, Awele slept off.

*****

It was a loud scream that woke her up—the high-pitched and frightened scream of a child. Heart pounding, Awele shot up from her bed like a bullet and listened, afraid she was having another nightmare.

"Jesus!" There was the scream again, and yes, the soulful wail. A child's voice pleading. "Please, sir, please! I beg you. In Jesus's name, please, please…!"

This was no dream. Something was happening in the courtyard. All sleep gone, Awele reached for her phone. It was almost 2:00 a.m. She listened again and heard the movement of hurried footsteps across the compound, muffled adult voices, and the whimper of a child. Awele ran to her window to look, but total darkness faced her. Oh yes, the barricade, she remembered, and retreated to her bed. Indistinct voices floated into her room again. She thought she heard a brief struggle. And a child's plaintive moan again.

She ran to the window in her living room from where she had watched Ma Edem earlier that day and looked out. Although darkness covered the compound, there were scraps of light from what looked like candles, borne by shadows that were flitting across the compound. For several minutes, she stretched her neck higher, peering through the cracks in the fence, but it was impossible to make out what was happening in the compound.

She realized then that this must have been the reason her landlord had constructed the fence. Something was going on in the compound, something he did not want her to see. But why, she asked herself. Why her in particular? Ritual sacrifices occurred every day, she wouldn't be the first or the last to witness animal sacrifice. Why was it important to him that she should not see his sacrifice?

Picking up her cell phone, Awele minimized the volume and quietly stole out of her house through the kitchen. She closed the door and crept toward the new fence. Her car was parked parallel to the wooden barricade, and it was easy for her to shuffle around it to the tiny opening she could see between the wooden panels. Soundlessly, she peered through and saw what appeared to be an idol worship ritual. She blinked several times to be sure she was seeing clearly. Five hooded figures, each holding a lit candlestick, stood in a semicircle in front of Edem's bungalow. In the middle of the circle was the witch doctor she had seen coming out of Edem's bungalow several weeks ago with a smoking basket. He was prancing about now, just as he had the last time she had seen him, making similar incantations. Those chants and grunts were now directed at the animal held down by two other men on the ground. He said something, took a gulp from the bottle in his hand, and sprayed the liquid from his mouth on the poor creature on the ground. As he spat on the animal, Awele heard it again, the cry of a child. That was when it hit her. This was no animal that was being sacrificed. This was a human being! A child!

She sucked in a deep breath and held her head to keep herself from fainting. No, it was not possible. Was her landlord trying to sacrifice a human being for Edem's healing? Was this what the great Chibala had told him? Hand over her mouth to stifle the cry that rose from her heart, she recalled the conversation she had overheard last week, and it all began to make sense. This was the ultimate sacrifice they had been talking about. Awele's legs began to shake. Horror seized her heart, and her breath quickened. Was she about to witness a human sacrifice? She racked her brain for details of the infamous conversation. This would not be the real sacrifice, she recalled. This was probably the part where Edem had to do something to prepare the "sheep for the slaughter." The actual sacrifice would occur at the witch doctor's shrine.

Scared and shaking, Awele stood rooted on the spot. Would they bring Edem out to touch the child and transfer his sickness on him as they did in the olden days or would they take the child into his chamber? The witch doctor continued his ceremony in low tones, and she could not make out what he was saying. But it was over very quickly, and she saw them bring white sheets and cover the child on the ground. The child was struggling, but in short order, the men restraining him down now lifted him up for the men in the circle to see.

Jesus! Awele gasped. This was the child in the news, the albino girl! This was Afam Izuwa's niece whom the whole nation has been looking for! She had been stripped naked and was not wearing her glasses, but Awele had no doubt that it was the same girl. While they held her up, the dibia filled his mouth with some liquid and sprayed it all over the girl. He dipped a short broom into a clay pot and spray-painted the child with a black liquid with the broom, all the while chanting incantations and springing around. And with every touch, the girl was moaning, begging, "Please! Please, sir! Please don't kill me! Please! I beg you, sir! Oh, Jesus!" Awele tried not to give in to a sudden disorientation as she turned toward her apartment. Blinded by her own tears, overcome by physical and emotional weakness, she leaned on the side of her Honda for several seconds before staggering to her kitchen door.

As she reached for the door, she felt a hand cover her mouth from behind and someone forcefully push her into her kitchen and shut the door behind them.

"Shh!" she heard her captor whisper. "Do not make any noise. Do not put on the light. Do not struggle. I am not here to hurt you. I need your help to save the life of that child."

"Ma Edem?" Awele asked, not quite sure with all the whispering.

"Yes, it's me. Sit on the floor. Don't let them see us. If my husband finds me here today, he will kill me."

The arms around her slackened and she turned to see the woman.

"Madam…"

"Shh. Listen, I did not know anything about this, okay? I had no idea. He told me it was his niece and I believed him. It was not until this night that he told me this was Chibala's offering. They will take her to the shrine at dawn."

"And kill her?"

"I don't know. Your guess is as good as mine what they will do to her. Sometimes, they keep the albinos in the shrines as servants to the priests. Even my husband does not know what the ultimate plan is. His part was to find her, prepare her for the sacrifice, and present her to the shrine."

"This is the preparation?"

"They are just starting."

"What happens next?"

"Edem has to defile her first."

"What?"

"You heard me. That is what they asked my husband to ensure. She is too pure. Edem has to sleep with her, make sure she is defiled tonight before she can be acceptable to the gods."

"Madam, she's just a child. She's eight years old."

"That is the wish of the gods."

"You mean Chibala? He's not a god."

"Look, let's not waste time. That child has been calling on Jesus since she was placed in my hands. She's been calling on him to save her. Even if she was not calling on Jesus, my conscience will not allow me to stand by and watch this happen. I need your help."

"Why don't you call the police? I will call them right now and put an end to this wickedness."

"Are you crazy? My husband was the commissioner of police. Do you think anyone will believe me? Do you want him to kill me?"

"But you have to do something."

"Yes. And you're going to help. Listen, I am going to find a way to bring that child to you this night, dead or alive, hopefully alive. You must find a way to smuggle her out of this compound this very night. My husband must not find her with you. If he does, your life will be over. Believe me, you don't want to get into his trouble."

"But why me, madam? Why do you want to involve me in this? I would rather just take my chances with the police."

"Because you are the one that preaches that with God all things are possible. Because that child has been calling on Jesus to come and rescue her since she's been in my house. This is his opportunity to do so and I am sure he wants you involved. Maybe that is why he sent you to this house after all, to save this little girl who believes in him. And I do not want that child's blood on my son's hand."

"Madam…"

"Shh. I must leave now. Do not go to sleep. Do not lock your kitchen door. I will bring her to you as soon as I can."

CHAPTER 30

Sleep is the cousin of death.

—African proverb

The buzzing of the cell phone startled Afam from a deep sleep. He had been dreaming of Ogugua and his father. In his dream, he saw them standing atop a hill beckoning to him to come up to them. He was at the foot of the hill, arguing with them, beckoning to them to come down to him. When they would not, he began to float through the air, moving upward until he was standing with them. A little child was holding Ogugua's hand—fair-complexioned, brown-eyed—and she was staring blankly at him. She had huge wings that flapped gently in the wind. She looked familiar. As he tried to place the child's face, Ogugua took the little girl's hand and put it in his hand.

He ignored the cell phone, trying desperately to continue in the dream, to talk to his father and hear his sister's voice and to ask for their help in locating Kamdi.

Kamdi!

That was Kamdi with the huge wings!

He shot up from the bed as the scene faded, surprised to find himself in his bedroom, on his bed, not sure if he was happy or sad that it had been a dream. He remained seated, blinking severally to fully wake up.

By the time he flicked the phone open, it had stopped buzzing.

He did not recognize the name from the caller ID, and he groaned in frustration. What kind of crazy person phoned you at 4.30 a.m.? He should have just let him finish his dream! Why was Kamdi with Ogugua and his father? Could it be that she was dead after all, that she had gone to rest with her mother and grandfather?

He laid down again and tried to go back to sleep, but the phone began to vibrate again, and this time, he picked it up and identified himself.

"Listen," an urgent voice whispered, "I know where your niece is being held, and why."

"Who is this?"

"You don't need to know who I am. Just listen."

"Are you asking for ransom?" He struggled to his feet, reaching for his house coat. "Is she okay? Can I speak with her? I'll pay you anything, anything you want, to release her to me. Just don't hurt her, please."

"Shh," the voice rebuked him impatiently. "I am not asking for any ransom. I just want to tell you what has happened to her."

"Is she alive?" Afam waited breathlessly.

"I don't know."

"What do you know?"

"I know a man who used to be a bad man, a headhunter for Chibala the witch doctor."

"Was he the one who kidnapped her?"

"No, but he told me what happened. Apparently, a woman, whom he suspects to be one of the daughters of Chibala, the witch doctor, told her father about your niece. She said the girl was standing between her and something she wanted dearly, and that she wanted the girl removed."

Afam's mind went to Vickie, but he kept his cool. Better to listen to what the stranger on the phone was saying.

"Removed or killed?"

"It doesn't matter. She wanted the albino out of the way."

"But why?"

"I don't know. You will have to ask her."

"Go on. I'm listening."

"At the same time, another man came to Chibala to consult about his sick son. Chibala told him the only thing that can cure his son is the sacrifice of an albino child to the gods."

Sacrifice? For the first time since the speculations about the possible murder of his niece, Afam had a terrible feeling in his gut that he had lost Kamdi forever. If what this caller was saying was true, then there was no more hope. Kamdi was gone. Her life had been taken violently. Sweet, innocent Kamdi. How could anyone look into those eyes and lift a knife against her? How would they carry it out—shoot her, behead her, slit her throat? His heart squeezed.

"Are you there, sir?"

"Yes. Please go on," he urged brokenly.

"Chibala's agents contacted the headhunter to go kidnap your niece and take her to the man for the sacrifice, but the headhunter refused. His conscience would not let him do it. When the agents insisted, he referred them to another man— Area Scatter. It was Area Scatter that kidnapped your niece. He has already passed the child to the man with the sick son at Ituandem."

"Who is this man? What is his name?"

"That I don't know. But the sacrifice is to take place at the high shrine at Ituandem. I don't know if they have done it already or not, but Area Scatter has delivered the child to the father of the sick child and received payment. Your best bet now is to locate the shrine in Ituandem and go there. With any luck, you can stop the sacrifice if she's still alive."

"Oh my god!"

"And another thing, you must not go to the police. Most of the top shots in government are clients of Chibala. Their hands are not clean. They will not let you fight Chibala. If you are not careful, they will kill you too."

Silence. Afam squeezed his hand to confirm he was not still dreaming.

"I was the one who called the police and told them about Area Scatter, but they ignored my tip. I had seen the girl with my two eyes, tied up in the boot of a Peugeot 505."

Afam groaned. He could not imagine it. *Kamdi?*

"How was she when you saw her?"

"I honestly can't tell you. I thought she was dead, but I heard later that she had been drugged."

As soon as the caller cut off, Afam did the only thing he could think of—he dialed Chief Martins's number.

CHAPTER 31

If you think you are too small to
make a difference, you have not spent
the night with a mosquito.

—African proverb

A wele tried not to give in to the fear that rattled inside her as she heard the commotion in the compound early the next morning. It started with raised voices—Pa Edem shouting at his wife, Ma Edem shouting back at him, just as loudly.

"I swear to God, I don't know where she has gone. I did not do anything with her, believe me. I was here all night. How could I have left and come back without your knowledge?"

The argument lasted for about five more minutes before she heard the man's footsteps running to the security gate. In the early morning, it was easy to hear her landlord directing the *mai-guard* to seal the gate, that no one could come in or go out without his permission. She stood very still, holding her breath, one eye at the door, another eye on Tokumbo's suitcase, one hand on the follow-up text message she had composed to send to her father, and another hand on her CD player, ready to press the record button at the appropriate time.

She did not have to wait for long. Hers was the only rental property in the compound so she knew he would head straight to her door. What she did not expect was the ferocity with which he kicked in her front door, breaking down the hinges and sending the door crashing into her living room. She did not expect him to be wielding a machete either, or to be accompanied by an armed police officer. She had never seen anyone with such a crazy look. She clicked on the send button on her phone, pressed down the record button on the cassette, and took a deep breath.

"Where is she?" he snarled.

"*Ah ah! Oga* landlord, are you okay? What are you doing here? Why did you kick down my door?"

"Search this house," he yelled at the policeman. "Search every nook and every corner. The child is in this house. I know it."

"What child, sir?" Awele asked. "What child are you looking for?"

"You know what child I am looking for!" He turned his crazy eyes to her. "You think I don't know you are behind her disappearance. You think I did not see the message you sent to Edem last night? May the gods strike you dead for interfering in my family affairs. May lightning strike you. *Agwo vukposik- wagianya ten times a day!* Stupid girl!"

"Ah, *Oga*, I don't know what you are talking about o! You people should leave my flat o! I am not owing you any rent. I am not owing you anything. How can you just come in and break down my door and start searching for something I don't even know about? It is not good o! I know my rights o! Hmm!"

"Shut up and listen very well. First, I will find this child. Then I will deal with you. By the time I am finished with you, even your parents will not recognize you. Foolish girl!"

Awele made to go after the policeman barging into her bedroom, but her landlord drew her back by her nightgown, ripping it from the side.

"*Henn... Oga*, look at what you have done!" she yelled. "You have torn my nightgown. I will shout o! I'm going to shout o!"

"If you shout, I will tear the whole dress to pieces and call on my boys to have their way with you right now. If you know what is good for you, you will just sit down on that chair and shut up. *Edem, don't do it for God's sake*, he mocked. Were those not your words? Is that not what you texted to Edem last night?"

"I...I..."

"What did you know about what Edem was supposed to do last night? How did you know about it?"

"*Oga*, I do not know what you are talking about. All I know is that Edem should be in the hospital. He is sick, and he is not going to get better staying at home. You've got to take him back to the hospital, sir. Please, sir!"

"I don't need your advice on how to look after my son. What I want to know is how you knew about last night and where you have hidden the child that the great Chibala has appointed for the sacrifice."

"Sacrifice, sir? What sacrifice? Who is Chibala? I have no idea what you are talking about. I don't know about any child. Who are these people? Is he the father of the child?"

"You cannot fool me, idiot! You know what I am talking about."

"I don't have any child with me. You can search every corner of my flat. You can even sweep the house if you like. You will not find any child with me."

Giving her a stare that would scare a lion, he left her and followed the officer into the bedroom. Awele followed. The officer was standing in front of Tokumbo's luggage. Her heart stopped as her eyes met the frightened gaze of Kamdi peeping from the slight opening she had left so that the girl could breathe. The wrapper she had tied over her head was still in place. But the officer had scattered more clothes around her head, taken down more clothes from Awele's closet, and piled them on top of the suitcase. How could he not have seen her? She stiffened as her eyes sought the officer's. Their gaze held, and her hand went to restrain the heart threatening to leap out from her chest. The officer had seen Kamdi! There was no doubt about it. She knew from the warning his eyes conveyed, the way he narrowed them and shook his head slightly at her. Summoning up courage, she continued her affronted disposition.

"So," she directed at the officer, hoping her voice would not give her away, "did you find what you were looking for? If you didn't, can I have some privacy in my home now? I want to use the toilet."

The man ignored her and turned to his master. "There's no one here, sir."

"Impossible!" Pa Edem declared. "Have you checked the toilet, the wardrobe, under the bed, under the table?"

"I've checked everywhere, sir. I've even checked inside her suitcase. I cannot find any child here."

"You are looking for a child in my suitcase? What do you take me for? A kidnapper?" Awele was outraged. The two men ignored her.

"Let me look by myself!"

So saying, Pa Edem went on his knees to peer under the bed. He swept his cutlass under the bed. Awele and the policeman exchanged another look. The policeman picked up the sheets and pillows from her bed, and piled them on top of the suitcase.

"She's got to be here. If not, where could she be?" A note of desperation had crept into Pa Edem's voice.

"But, *Oga*, who are you looking for? This Chibala that you are talking about, is it her child that is missing?"

"Youth corper, mind yourself! Do not provoke me further."

"I'm sorry, sir," she mumbled. She heaved a quiet sigh of relief when they moved from the bedroom and trooped back to the living room.

"I've got to find her. I've got to…aha, maybe she has hidden her in her car. Hand over your car keys now!"

Awele gave the keys to the policeman and waited with her agitated landlord while he went to look. She kept her eyes down so he would not read her fear. She heard her car door open and close.

"The car is empty, sir," the policeman said, as he came back in. "Maybe the child has run away into the village," the policeman suggested, but Pa Edem only glared at him. "Or maybe not, sir. The gateman would have seen her."

"Not if she left last night. I gave the gateman the night off. He came back early this morning."

"Let me put my men on it, sir. She could not have gone too far. If, as you say, she was wounded and tired, she may even be lying in a gutter somewhere now."

"Okay. Let's go. Hurry! I've got to find her. As for you, youth corper." He turned those menacing eyes at her. She did not flinch. "Do not leave this compound today. I will deal with you when I get back."

Pa Edem left first, and she saw the policeman carefully drop the car key behind him as he followed. She waited until he was a safe distance away before picking up the keys. Then she shouted after them.

"*Oga* Landlord, this one wey you come break my door this early morning, what am I supposed to do? I'm not going to stay o! I cannot stay in a house without a door. I'm leaving. Tell the gateman to let me pass o!'

She breathed a sigh of relief as soon as she lost sight of them. She checked her time. It was not even seven o'clock. She drew her curtains shut and ran to Tokumbo's luggage. "They are gone. Are you okay in there?" she whispered.

"Yes," Kamdi responded. "I stayed like a statue...and I prayed."

"Good girl. Just give me a few more minutes, and I will get you out of here. You can relax now but try not to make a sound until we leave, okay? I have to roll the suitcase to the car so nobody will suspect me. Are you still okay to stay in there for a few more minutes?"

She ran to her sitting room and switched on her radio, turning the volume high to ensure no one would hear her talking to the child. When she went to check on the girl again, she was shaking, and her eyes were wide with fright.

"That policeman—he saw me. He opened the suitcase, and he saw me. He looked at me." Kamdi was shivering.

"I know he did. But he didn't say anything. That was a miracle, Kamdi. God is really watching over you."

"Are they...are they coming back?"

"Don't worry about it, okay? We will be out of here before they come back. Just stay still for me, okay? Like a statue...no movement."

She picked up her phone and dialed her father's number. When he didn't answer, she slapped it shut and ran to her room and pulled more stuff into another suitcase. She took the CD from the player, put it in her purse; then she reached into a tiny pot on her counter where she had hid her spare keys.

"I'm taking you to the car now," she whispered to the girl in the suitcase. She zipped up the suitcase, leaving a tiny opening so she could breathe. "Remember...no sound...and no movement..."

Awele blessed Dr. Ben in her heart as she carried the luggage to the trunk of her Honda CRV. He had not only repaired her car while she had been ill, he had also given her a full gas tank.

Thank you, Lord, that you make all things work together for the good of those that love you, for those who are called according to your purpose. This is your purpose, Lord. It is your doing.

She rolled Tokumbo's suitcase to the car and placed it in the back seat. Then she brought out the second suitcase and her purse, and dumped them on the passenger seats. She ran back to grab her bedsheets and pillows, which she scattered on top of the luggage in the back seat and hopped into the car. She had to wiggle the car out from its spot behind the wooden barricade, but she was a good driver, and after multiple turns, she was facing the security gate.

She waited, but the *mai guard* did not show up. She jumped out of the car to call him, but he was nowhere to be seen. Inside the gatehouse, she found a wire rope holding five keys and took them to try and unlock the padlock at the gate. While trying the keys, her hand shook so badly that she dropped the bunch two times. Finally, she heard the click and ran to open the gate wide. As she got back into her car, she saw the security man running from a distance, shouting after her. Smiling, she lifted a hand and waved at him as she put the car in drive and accelerated.

Twenty minutes later, she was knocking on Dr. Ben's front door.

"You've got to help me, Ben," she begged and gave him a quick download of what she had witnessed last night and what had transpired this morning in her flat. "They will be after me by now. I know it."

"You crazy girl," he admonished. "What have you got yourself into now? I warned you to stay clear of that man. I told you he was dangerous."

"Please don't be offended. I didn't know where else to go to, I didn't know who else could help. I just need somewhere safe for us until my father comes for me. I've contacted him. If he is not already on the flight to Ituandem right now, he will be very soon."

"So where is the girl now?"

"She's in the car, still in Tokumbo's suitcase. Please hurry, Ben. If they come here and find my car, they will suspect that you are giving me shelter, and we will both be in trouble."

He ran a frustrated hand through his head. "So, what do you want me to do? I really do not want to get involved in this."

"Can you drive your car out from your garage so I can park mine inside? Please, Ben. And can you tell me how I can take care of this child until my father arrives? She's got bruises all over her body, and she's running a wild temperature, and she's very scared."

CHAPTER 32

*A child does not die because her
mother's breasts are dry.*

—African proverb

That same morning, mobile police officers, also known as MOPOL, under instruction from the police headquarters in Abuja, made two simultaneous arrests. Vickie was arrested in Lagos, on her way to the airport, and Rachel was picked up just outside her home at Oloibiri Street in Port Harcourt.

Nigerians have a saying: it is a fearful thing to fall into the hands of MOPOL. Vickie and her sister discovered the truth of that saying that morning when the officers began their torture process, which they called routine interrogation. The two women soon began to sing like canary birds.

"It was Rachel's idea," Vickie cried through bloodied lips as the officers in Lagos took turns kicking and hitting her.

"It was our father's idea," Rachel confessed when she felt she would die from the whacking and slapping by the officers in Port Harcourt. Her eyes were black and swollen. Blood gushed from cuts and bruises on her face and neck. She spoke slowly, "In our family, we forbid albinos."

"You what?" cried a MOPOL officer, slapping her across her already swollen face. Her teeth rattled. "Are you God? Who gave you the authority to forbid another human being?"

She cried out in pain.

"Our father is the *eze nmoo*..." her words were slurred, and she spoke slowly. "The chief high priest...of the great Chibala... Our family is forbidden from associating with albinos... We cannot sleep under the same roof as an albino...we cannot eat from the same pot as albino...we cannot marry anybody with albino blood..."

"And if you do?"

"If we do, we will die... The gods will strike us dead."

"Then why don't you leave them alone when you see them? Why do you want to kill them? Why kill the girl?"

"My sister... Vickie was supposed to marry Afam... She cannot marry him unless the albino is dead... That was the condition the gods...gave to *eze nmoo*. The child...must...die."

She was slipping into unconsciousness. Her eyes were closing, her voice growing fainter.

One of the officers spat on the ground and shook his head in revulsion. "That your god is very wicked!"

The four officers questioning Rachel relented only after she gave them her father's phone number and residential address.

Two hours later, MOPOL officers picked up the *eze nmoo*, Chibala's high priest, Vickie's father. They also arrested Area Scatter and MoBoy.

But when they arrived Magaji Estates, shortly after ten that morning, Pa Edem was nowhere to be found. So they arrested his wife.

*****

250

Although the journey from Port Harcourt to Ituandem was five hours by road or one hour by flight, Afam did not want to take chances with the airplane. The first flight would leave at noon. By then, he intended to be at the shrine of Chibala in Ituandem. So very early that morning, along with Binta and Okee, he set off.

They didn't know the way to the shrine at Ituandem, didn't know what to do when they got there, but all three were determined not to sit idly by if there was a chance they could find the missing girl and stop the sacrifice.

They discussed their strategies extensively as they traveled past Aba, Okigwe, Afikpo, and Abakiliki toward Ituandem. Okee suggested that since they could not go to the police station for help, they could go to the Ituandem Motor Park and hire two or three young men to go along with them to the shrine. The hirelings would come in handy if the confrontation got physical.

"We can raise an alarm if we see her at the shrine," Binta suggested. "If we raise enough alarm to gather a crowd, they may get scared and leave her and run away."

Afam did not say anything. He had an ominous feeling in his gut that something momentous had to happen today in the search for Kamdi—either good or bad. This was probably the last opportunity to find her, dead or alive. If she was not found in the next couple of hours, it could very well be over.

They were halfway to Ituandem when his phone rang. He recognized Chief Martins's number and immediately pressed the green button. "Hello, sir."

"Where are you?" there was an urgency in the chief's voice. "I've been trying to get you."

"I'm on my way to Ituandem, sir."

"Are you driving? Are you by yourself?"

"I'm driving, but I have two friends with me, sir."

"Very good. I need you to pull over. I will hold on until you do. I have news for you."

There was a pause as Afam veered off the road. He could feel the blood leaving his body—first his face, then his chest and arms. *Kamdi must be dead*, he thought. His legs shook as he held on to his cell phone with his left hand and the steering wheel with his right. He switched off the engine.

Please, God! Help me, please.

*****

Awele's heart jumped when she heard the muffled crying from the room where Kamdi lay sleeping. She raced in to find the girl tossing on the bed, tears streaming down her cheeks, mumbling incoherently. Awele felt her forehead with the back of her hand and confirmed that the child was still running a high fever. *And no wonder*, she thought to herself, *who wouldn't fall ill after the trauma the poor girl had been through?*

She went to the bathroom, filled a bowl with cold water, and grabbed a face towel. When she sat on the bed, the girl registered her presence, and her eyes flew open.

"Shh…it's okay." Awele bent to kiss her brow. She could not help it—the sympathy she felt for this helpless child was so strong it stunned her. Maybe it was because Kamdi reminded her of her little sister. Or because of all that the little girl had suffered. If there was ever a child in whose life Awele knew God was working, it had to be Kamdi Garuba. She considered herself blessed to have been a part of the story of her divine deliverance. "Shh…you're going to be okay."

Awele dipped the towel in the cold water and began dabbing her face and neck. Earlier, when she had bathed the girl, she had been mindful of the bruises on her thin ankle and hands, where she had been bound with ropes, and done her best not to cause her more pain. Dr. Ben had said she had all the signs of emaciation and that he would need to get her to a hospital as soon as possible for blood tests and x-rays. But Awele had begged him to let them stay indoors for that day, at least until her father arrived from Abuja or until they could be certain they were free from Pa Edem's pursuit.

She knew that the bruises on the girl's body will heal with time, and that with good nutrition, she will regain weight. But she could not say the same about the emotional bruises. The girl had not said much to her, but the way her large myopic eyes followed her everywhere, suspiciously, as though she still couldn't trust her, caused Awele some concern. It could take a long time for her to trust again.

She had finally spoken to her father that morning, and he had given her the cheering news that most of the culprits behind Kamdi's abduction had been rounded up—all except Pa Edem who had conveniently disappeared. Although Ma Edem had been apprehended instead, Awele was confident that when she told the police the role the woman had played in securing Kamdi's freedom, they would release her.

Something about Awele's ministrations seemed to convince the albino girl that she did not mean to hurt her. Awele watched her slowly relax and close her eyes. Her breathing was gradually returning to normal. Although the fever continued to burn through her body, and her eyes became drowsy, she still managed to keep them fixed on Awele.

Awele wondered what the young girl was thinking. She hoped she could she see in her eyes how sorry she was for all the terror she had endured since her abduction. When she stood up to return the bowl to the bathroom, Kamdi cried out and reached for her hand. She felt a surge of hope as she sat down again and spoke gently to the girl.

"You will be okay. All the people who wanted to hurt you have been arrested by the police. You don't need to be afraid anymore."

She tried to gently prise the girl's hands from hers, but Kamdi held even tighter, kicking her legs between the sheets in protest. Awele dropped the bowl by the bedside and leaned and spoke again, softly, into the girl's ear.

"I'm not leaving you. I just need to grab those medicine bottles on that table for you. The doctor wants you to drink them so you can get well and strong before you go back to your uncle and brothers. Can you let go of my hand so I can pick them up and come back? I'll be really quick."

Slowly, the girl's hand slackened, and she rushed to bring the medicine bottles. While she was at it, she grabbed her Bible from the table as well. She would sit with the girl and read to her until she slept again. She also picked up a pink flowered night gown she had brought out from her suitcase this morning in her haste to escape Pa Edem. The gown was too small for her and would be too big for the little girl, but she needed a change of clothes, and this would do for now.

After administering the medicines and changing her into the nightgown, Awele pulled a chair beside the bed. She would read to her one of her favorite books of the Bible—the book of Ruth.

But when she opened her Bible, the picture of Afam Izuwa that her mother had sent her fell out from the pages and landed on the floor. Awele's heart beat with excitement, and her hand shook as she showed the photograph to the child, watching her face closely to gauge her reaction. Large, uncoordinated eyes squinted at the photograph for several seconds before Kamdi grasped it from Awele's hands. She clutched the photograph with her two hands, holding it to her heart as the tears started to pour down her cheeks.

"Uncle 'Zuwa! Uncle 'Zuwa!" Kamdi repeated over and over again. Awele brushed away her own tears and smiled. The girl was still holding tight onto her uncle's photograph when the drugs Awele had given her began to take effect. Awele let her hold onto the picture as she fell asleep.

*****

The message button on Awele's phone flashed two hours later, and she hurried out to the sitting room and stationed herself beside the window. She heard the gate open three minutes later and saw Dr. Ben's car drive in, followed by a black SUV. As soon as she saw her father step out of the car, Awele ran downstairs to fling the front door open and throw herself into her father's arms.

"Daddy!"

"Oh, my daughter! Awele! Are you okay?"

"Oh yes, Daddy. I'm fine," she beamed at him.

"Let me look at you!" He held her back for a few seconds before hugging her tight. "May God bless you, my child. May God bless you. Ben has told me how brave you have been. I am so proud of you. You have done very well."

"Oh, Daddy, I didn't do anything. The Lord worked out everything. He put me in the right place at the right time for that child. You need to see her, sir. She's the sweetest child that you ever saw, but her spirit has been badly wounded."

Just then, she remembered that they were not alone. The car that drove in after Dr. Ben's had parked, and three people had come to stand beside her father. Her heart seemed to skip a beat as she recognized Afam Izuwa. It would have been impossible not to recognize the person whose photograph she had been looking at only a couple of hours ago. Their eyes met, and for several seconds, she seemed unable to break eye contact with him. It flitted through her mind that the photograph didn't do him justice. He looked so much more attractive in real life.

Her father did a quick introduction, and without any fuss, she turned and led everyone upstairs. They were all eager to see Kamdi to confirm that she was truly all right, and Awele was just as eager to put everyone out of their misery.

"She's been ill," she explained, as they stopped in the sitting room. "Fever, shakes, and nightmares. She was sleeping when I left her."

Dr. Ben turned to Afam from the fridge door, where he had headed to bring out cold drinks from the fridge. "I think it would be best that I check on her first before you go in. I won't be long."

Afam nodded, and Awele followed the doctor out of the room. While they waited, Binta poured the drinks into glasses and passed them around. Chief Martins was beaming from ear to ear, rehashing again the events of the day—the numerous arrests and the confessions. He was full of praise for his friend, the inspector general of police, who had orchestrated the arrests. Okee joined him, lamenting the depth of corruption in the state police bureaus.

"All the leads were there," Okee said. "The police knew who was responsible, but they wouldn't investigate. They were prepared to sacrifice a little girl so that they would not expose themselves and their friends. Wickedness in high places is what it is. It doesn't get worse than this."

Afam did not say much. The news of Kamdi's rescue had disorientated him and his emotions were still reeling with shock. It was as if he was waiting to see her before he could believe that she was indeed safe. He folded his arms across his chest, squeezing his hands together in tight fists, hearing the buzz of conversation around him but not really following.

The chief's voice broke when he recalled the moment he got the text message from Awele telling him that she had rescued the child and that her life was in danger from her landlord.

"That was the worst moment of my life. I know how ruthless these characters can be, and I was afraid. I've never felt so helpless or vulnerable in my life. If anything had happened to my daughter, I don't know what I would have done with myself. Kind of how you may have been feeling this past week, Afam."

Afam nodded. He still had goosebumps all over his body. His mind had not fully grasped the message that the nightmare was finally over.

"I was able to contact the IG just in time," Chief Martins continued. "He postponed his meetings today to focus on this case. I was praying all the while that he would act on time to save Awele from her wicked landlord. And I was praying that God would grant her wisdom and courage, and show her a way of escape."

Binta's eyes lit up in response. "And he did! God answers prayers. He's still doing miracles!"

"As for that Mr. Magaji—can you believe that man used to be the police commissioner in this very state? When Awele came here for youth service, I thought she would be safe living in his home. I did not know it would be the opposite, that I was throwing her into the lion's den. If he is wise, he will surrender soon, for his own sake. There are many people waiting to exact jungle justice on him. He doesn't have many friends in the civilian population of Ituandem."

They heard coughing from the room, and everyone went quiet and listened. Then they heard footsteps, and Afam spotted Awele as she came through the door.

"She's still very sick, but Dr. Ben has given her more drugs, and he says you can see her now, but not everyone at once so she is not overwhelmed. Mr. Izuwa can come in first. I'll come for you next," she directed at Binta.

*****

Afam wanted to race across the room to where his niece lay on the bed, but he couldn't do it, couldn't take his eyes off her for fear she would disappear and everything about the past twenty-four hours would turn out to be nothing more than a haunting dream. He was shocked at how thin she had become, and he inhaled deeply to steady his emotions. Without her glasses, she looked vastly different, but it was her all right.

Dear Lord, thank you. It is her…it's really Kamdi. You came through for us. You answered everyone's prayers. Thank you, Lord.

SON, DO YOU NOW BELIEVE?

Afam exhaled softly. He shook his head at the wonder of it all. *Yes. Lord. I believe.*

He slowed his pace as he approached the bed. Awele quickly moved to kneel beside the bed, and, watching him with an encouraging smile, she whispered softly into Kamdi's ears.

Kamdi turned slowly and squinted in his direction.

What happened next was beyond his imagination. The moment Kamdi recognized him, she let out a scream, shot out of bed and straight into his arms.

"Uncle 'Zuwaa!" she screamed, her words coming out like trapped cries escaping from the recesses of her soul. "Uncle 'Zuwaa!"

He held her tight, hugging, kissing, and pressing her face into his shoulder. She held on just as tight, and her tears fell like a torrent against his shirt.

Awele's tears fell silently. She lifted her hand to her chest to still the joy and excitement bubbling in her heart. She was sobbing and smiling at the same time. Dr. Ben looked on with a smile.

Afam lifted Kamdi's face from his shoulder for a few seconds to examine her through his own tears, but she buried her face in his shoulders once more and held even tighter.

"Uncle 'Zuwaa!"

The power of her tears reminded him of how she had cried the first day he saw her, held just like this in Binta's arms. He felt the shivers that ran through her thin body, felt the heat of the fever that was coursing through her, heard the breath that came in short gasps, and he lifted another silent thanksgiving upward. What a strong girl she was—a survivor, for sure. Life had handed her yet another adversity, and she had come through with courage and resilience. For several minutes, he sat on the bed and held her wrapped in his arms, rocking her until the hiccups subsided, smoothing his hand over her back and her hair, whispering comforting words.

"I will lift up my eyes to the hills…" he tried to recall the psalm. "Where does my help come from?…my help comes from the Lord, the maker of heaven and earth…he who keeps Kamdi never sleeps nor slumbers," he whispered. "You are a miracle child, Kamdi. Your God is watching over you…all the time…"

The psalm reached her, and the sobs died down. Finally, she looked up at him, studying his face and cradling his head with her hands.

"John? Peter?" Her response was a question.

"They are waiting for you at home," he told her, smiling. "And there's someone else outside waiting to see you. She came all the way from Scotland when she heard you were missing."

"Auntie Binta?"

There was only one word Awele could use to describe the joy that shone through Kamdi when her uncle nodded: priceless.

CHAPTER 33

And a little child shall lead them...

Ten weeks after Kamdi's rescue, Afam Izuwa sat at the end of the church pew, dressed in the ceremonial *kaftan* lace, and glanced down at his young charges. Peter and John sat next to him, then his brother, Uwadiegwu, and Ebele. Kamdi sat between Ebele and his mother, her small fingers linked tightly with his mother's.

Phidelia was peering through her glasses, unsuccessfully leafing through her Bible. She bent down and whispered something to Kamdi, and the young girl giggled, lifting her free hand to her mouth before reaching across to help her grandmother find the page she was looking for. Watching them huddled so closely had become the new normal, much to everyone's delight.

Neither Afam nor any of his siblings ever imagined that Phidelia Izuwa could change so drastically, or that such a U-turn was even possible with her, but she was really a changed woman. Her selfishness and mean-spiritedness had mostly given way to demonstrations of kindness that no one could ever have associated with her, and Afam was struck daily by how she had taken Kamdi under her wings, and how the little girl was blossoming under her care. Miracles still happen.

Soon after Kamdi was discharged from the hospital, Phidelia had suggested that the family should hold a special thanksgiving service to celebrate her rescue from her abductors, and everyone had agreed. However, none of them had been prepared for the grand ceremony she began to plan. She had hired a huge hall, sent out invitations, hired caterers, hired a popular music band, bought clothes for everyone in the family, commissioned a special liberation cake, and spared no expense on any single detail for the lavish celebration. This was why they were all gathered at the Resurrection Hope Cathedral this morning—along with over three hundred guests—all dressed in their Sunday best.

Afam glanced at Kamdi again, admiring her special pink and white lace dress. Every other member of the family wore the blue color of the same lace material, but Kamdi's was different because this was really her special day. Not only had she survived a terrible ordeal, her experience was responsible for his entire family's spiritual restoration. And she had become a mini celebrity. Her story had been in the media for several weeks after her rescue and had in many ways exposed the corruption in the government and the deceitful practices of witch doctors. Because of her, the Federal Minister of Culture had convened a national dialogue on diversity and inclusion in the society, and citizens were speaking up about the fate of albinos and other marginalized groups all over the country. Watching now as she listened attentively to whatever her grandmother was telling her, Afam remembered Ogugua and knew that she would be pleased if she could see them now.

Someone tapped him on the shoulder, and he looked up to see Okee.

"Ol' boy, you guys have shut down Port Harcourt today!" His friend was beaming down at him. "I had to park two blocks away and walk down here. Any idea how many people are here?"

Afam stood up to shake his hand and to look around the cathedral. It was true—the entire auditorium was packed full, and there was still a crowd outside. Word had gone out about the thanksgiving service, and many people who had heard about the modern-day miracle had come to see the girl for themselves.

"Have you read the breaking news?" Okee's voice broke into his thoughts. "Hot off the press from the *Guardian* news online."

"No, what breaking news?"

"They found him dead."

"Who?"

"Mr. Magaji! The man who abducted your niece."

"The landlord? When? What happened?"

"Apparently, according to this report, the police got a tip that he was holed up in a house somewhere in Ondo state. They raided the house and found his dead body. He had been stabbed several times. It looked like ritual killing. Some parts of his body had been removed."

"Oh no!"

"Oh yes!" Okee retorted. "Poetic justice if it is true. See, the news is all over the internet right now. It's trending like wildfire. Maybe that is why so many people have turned up for the service today. There are throngs of people outside, most of who I'm sure you guys never invited."

Afam quickly switched on his iPhone and read the news for himself. There was also an update on the man's sick son. His mother had taken him to a hospital in India for treatment, and the HIV was responding to treatment. *There is a God indeed*, he shook his head in awe and wonder.

Afam looked around the church auditorium again. A naturally reserved person, he did not have too many friends, so his personal guests were only a dozen or so business acquaintances. Still, he recognized some members of his extended family who had chattered a bus from Amakama to attend the thanksgiving celebration. He assumed most of the guests were his mother's, but he could not be too sure. There were just too many people in attendance.

About four rows from where he sat was the Martins family. In two short months, he had grown increasingly attached to his late father's business partner, grateful every day for his help in finding Kamdi, when it seemed that all was lost, and for bringing her abductors to justice. He had spent several minutes on the phone with Betty Martins also and already felt as if he knew her quite well. The couple had arrived from Abuja last night with their three young children. When Afam asked about Awele, he was told she had returned from youth service three nights prior and had been too tired to join them on the trip to Port Harcourt.

He did not quite believe that. He had the feeling she was trying to avoid him. Since the day he had picked up Kamdi from her care at Ituandem, they had spoken only three times, and on each occasion, the conversation had been awkward and stilted. The first time was one week after the rescue, when he had called to thank her. She had listened politely, pointedly diverted the thanks he was expressing to God, and an awkward silence had ensued. When he did not know what else to say, they said their good-byes and hung up. When he dialed her number a week later, she hadn't been less formal. Kamdi had just been discharged from the hospital and had asked about her, so he had placed the call. He had started the conversation but soon ran into a block of silence, so he passed the phone over to Kamdi and that was it. Two weeks ago, he had called to invite her to the thanksgiving celebration, but she had been hurrying to some end of youth service event and could not talk. He was beginning to think that maybe she did not like him, and he did not understand why.

Someone struck a high-pitched bell, effectively calling everyone to order. When everywhere became quiet, the worship leader of Resurrection Hope Cathedral moved to the center of the podium. He lifted his hands and the congregation rose to its feet. Then he opened his Bible and began to read from Isaiah 43.

> But now thus says the Lord, he who created you, he who formed you: "Fear not, for I have redeemed you; I have called you by name, you are mine. When you pass through the waters, I will be with you; and through the rivers, they shall not overwhelm you; when you walk through fire you shall not be burned, and the flame shall not consume you. For I am the Lord your God, the Holy One of Israel, your Savior. Because you are precious in my eyes, and honored, and I love you, I give men in return for you, peoples in exchange for your life. Fear not, for I am with you."

"What more can I say, brethren?" the worship leader's voice boomed throughout the cathedral. "This day, this Scripture has been fulfilled before our eyes. We are all witnesses!"

"Amen! Praise the Lord! We are witnesses!" the congregation responded.

And with that, the thanksgiving service began.

*****

Except for the speeches, the main agenda for the reception was lunch. The ushers did a great job of seating the hundreds of guests and ensuring everyone had enough to eat and drink. As the chief host, Afam spent the afternoon shaking hands and retelling the story of Kamdi's rescue from abduction. Many times, Kamdi stood with him as he greeted the guests, and she obliged everyone who wanted to take a selfie with her. She seemed to be enjoying the attention. Some of Peter and John's friends from school were in attendance, and they spent the time at the reception together, joking and playing.

After lunch, the musicians struck the chords to some traditional music, and the dancing began. First, there was a family dance, then everyone hit the floor. Afam scanned the crowd and saw Kamdi chatting animatedly with a girl about her age, whom he recognized as Chief Martins's younger daughter. The cloud of self-pity and reticence that had shrouded her since she came to live with him had finally lifted, and she was becoming more confident with every new day. She was talking more, laughing more, and playing more. He figured that this was partly because of all the attention she had been garnering, but he hoped that it was mostly because she knew that everybody loved her.

Many of the guests were on the dance floor, singing to popular songs, swaying to the beat of the talking drum, and showing off their dance moves. It was getting hot and stuffy in the hall, and Afam needed fresh air. He found a beverage cart and took a bottle of cold water before stepping out to the balcony, where he found a quiet place near the back of the hall. Out there he took a break from the pressing crowd and watched the traffic on Stadium Road.

The day had been wonderful, everything had been perfect. Well, almost everything. He still could not get over the fact that Awele Martins had deliberately absented herself from the occasion. Why didn't she like him? Whatever had he done that had angered her so much that she did not want anything to do with him? He didn't think he was that bad looking. And he had liked what he had seen of her that day. If circumstances had been different, if they had met in better conditions, could they have become friends by now? Could their relationship have gone the way their mothers had hoped?

He would go after her, he decided. After the celebrations, after everyone and every house guest had left, he would take a trip to Abuja, and he will not leave until they talked. Really talked.

Afam lifted the bottle, and as he took a sip of the water, he sensed someone come into the balcony behind him. Before he had time to look up, he heard his name.

"Good evening, Mr. Afam Izuwa."

He recognized that voice. Slowly, as though in a trance, he set the water bottle on a nearby table and turned, and his heart seemed to stop. Awele Martins...

Nigerian party attire had never looked more beautiful on any woman than it did on this beautiful black girl. Her *iro* and *buba* were the color of coral, made from a lace fabric which he thought looked exquisite on her. Her beige head tie and subtle makeup had him shaking his head in admiration. Her high-heeled shoes caught his eyes because they were a sparkling silver shade, matching very well with her silver handbag. She looked like royalty.

"Are you not the host of the party?" She locked eyes with him and came closer. "What are you doing outside the hall by yourself?"

He could not look away from her nervous smile, and before common sense could stop him, he was shaking her hand, grabbing her into his arms and hugging her close. The singing and dancing in the hall faded as he held her, wondering if she could feel his fast-beating heart.

"Would you believe me if I said I was just thinking about you?" he finally answered her question. "Wondering what I ever did to make you dislike me."

At this, she leaned back and studied him, biting at her lips and trying to get serious. And he studied her, too, taking in the full red lips, the smiling wide eyes fringed with thick, long lashes, the straight nose, and the soft fragrance of her perfume. She really was beautiful. He held her eyes for a moment. "Where did I go wrong?"

"Afam Izuwa..." she started, paused, and looked away. His tug brought her back to face him. "Afam...I will not be part of an arranged marriage..."

"What?" His bright eyes shined into hers, searching the deep parts of her soul.

"Or an arranged anything," she added hastily.

His gaze held hers again, and then he understood. "You think my interest in you is because of our meddling mothers? You think that is why I have been calling you?"

She nodded bravely.

"You couldn't be farther from the truth," he said, not breaking eye contact. "You're so wrong..."

"But..." she paused.

"But what?" he asked again, encouraging her to explain, listening closely to hear what her words were not saying. In his ears, her voice was more melodious than the music streaming from the loudspeakers in the reception hall.

"My mother sent me a letter and photographs. She said you were interested in me and..." she paused again, biting her lips in embarrassment.

"So did my mother. She told me about you probably long before your mother told you about me. She sent me photographs too... Like you, I am not interested in an arranged relationship, and, from what I knew of my mother, I was prepared to dislike whoever she recommended for me. In fact, I ripped the photos into shreds and threw them away. I was not planning to like you. I was not planning to follow up with you. Until… well, there was a divine intervention, I think."

She opened her eyes wide. What was he saying?

Afam could tell that this was a difficult conversation for her and admired her even more for sticking with it.

Awele swallowed, as though there was a lump in her throat that made talking difficult.

"Gratitude doesn't work for me either," she whispered firmly, watching him closely. "If you must give thanks, give it all to the Lord who sent me and enabled me to rescue your niece. Like I keep saying, I was at the right place at the right time and did what any other person would have done in the same circumstances."

That was debatable, but he was not going to argue with her. He was still looking at her, still searching her eyes with that focused intensity.

"That is fair, I guess. So, if it is not gratitude, what works for you?"

She found a spot on his face and stared at it, breaking the eye lock. "You don't know me."

"I would like to. And I want you to get to know me."

"Why?"

"If I said it's because I think you are beautiful, smart, and courageous, that would be only part of the reason."

She closed her eyes, feeling embarrassed, biting back trembling lips.

"If I said it is because our families think that we would be good together, that would still be only part of the reason. And if I said it is because Kamdi has been asking for you, wondering when she will see you again, that would also be partly true."

He smiled at her closed eyes and slightly shook her shoulders so she could open them. He wanted to look into her eyes at his next words.

"The truth is I have been thinking about you a lot. And I like the way I feel when I think about you. I think there is something between us that is worth pursuing, if you will agree."

There.

He had said the thing he had been thinking about since the day he met her. That maybe it was not just their mothers, that perhaps it was God who was leading them toward one another. Of all the people in Ituandem God could have prepared and used to save Kamdi from certain death, it had been Awele Martins, the same woman whose praises his mother had been singing for weeks! He could never have made that one up by himself.

Their eyes held again, and she searched his face. "Really?" her voice trembled.

He resisted the urge to brush his knuckles against her cheekbone, the urge to get too familiar too quickly. "Yes, really."

For several seconds, she continued to search his face. He was encouraged by the smile he could see lurking at the corners of her mouth.

"So, what do you say?" he asked.

"To what?" she asked.

"To my getting to know you, to your getting to know me, to our exploring this thing between us and seeing where it will lead us to."

She took her time answering, and when she did, his heart soared.

"If I said yes, how would we do that? Where would we start from?"

As though in response, the deejay changed the music booming from the hall into a lively pop tune. Afam's heart bubbled with happiness and he silently gave thanks.

"Maybe the first thing you need to know about me is that I am probably one of the best dancers you have ever seen."

The sound of her giggle set his heart racing faster. *Dear Lord!...* He let her go for a moment, only to turn around and stretch his right hand toward where she stood watching him.

"Can I have the honor of this dance with you, Miss Martins?"

Awele giggled again and put her hand in his. His hand tightened around her fingers as he bent and kissed the back of her proffered hand. Then he tucked it in his elbow and led her into the hall and to the dance floor. The crowd made room for them, gathered around them, and cheered loudly as they danced.

Phidelia Izuwa and Betty Martins saw them from where they sat at the high table and gave each other a high five.

—— DISCUSSION QUESTIONS ——

1. Have you ever been impacted by terrorism? How did this influence your life? What are some ways we can assist people we know who have been victims of terrorism attacks or other tragedies?
2. Give examples of people who are different from you. How do you relate to them? Do you treat them differently? What does this tell you about human nature?
3. Are you or any member of your family involved in a transcultural relationship? What effect has this had on your extended family relationships?
4. Do you believe in *juju* or in supernatural powers? On what evidence?
5. Ogugua Garuba was estranged from her family for most of her life. Do you have a family member who is estranged now, whom you need to reach out to today?
6. There is a proverb for each of the chapters in this book. Which one is your favorite? Why?
7. How can you advocate for anyone you know who is being bullied because of their physical attribute(s)?

· GLOSSARY OF NIGERIAN WORDS ·
(in alphabetic order)

1. Adire—tie and dye fabric
2. Agwovukposikwagianya—curse word, showing hatred
3. Akara—bean cake
4. Akpati—suitcase, luggage
5. Ankara—Nigerian print fabric
6. Area boys—thugs
7. Baba—respectful term for an old wise man
8. Boko Haram—terrorist organization operating in Northern Nigeria
9. Dibia—doctor
10. Egusi—melon seeds
11. Eze nmoo—high priest in a juju temple
12. Garri—cassava flour
13. Haba!—exclamation of disbelief
14. Iro and buba—traditional wrapper and blouse worn by women
15. Iroko—tree believed to have magical powers
16. Juju—traditional spiritual belief in magical powers that are practiced with charms, amulets, and fetish practices associated with ancestral and other spirits
17. Kekenapepe—tricycle taxis
18. Mai-guard—personal security guard usually living and stationed at the gate house of properties
19. Mama-put—roadside barbecue joint

20. Mammywota—river goddess
21. Mumu—foolish, gullible behavior
22. Naija—pidgin English for Nigeria
23. National Youth Service Corps (also Youth Service)—one-year mandatory service for Nigerian graduates
24. Nko—expression added to a statement, always in question form, to confirm a question
25. Nne—mother
26. Nzu—white chalk made from limestones
27. Oga—sir
28. Ojukwu—ancestral spirit
29. Okada—motorcycle taxi
30. Okazi (ukazi)—vegetable
31. Oturugbeke—exclamation of surprise and concern
32. Owumiri—river goddess
33. Oyibo—slang for white person, or albinos
34. Tufiakwa!—exclamation of disgust
35. Udara—African star apple
36. Ugu—pumpkin leaves
37. Wahala—trouble
38. Walahi talahi—a solemn oath, I swear to God!

39. Wetin?—what?

ABOUT THE AUTHOR

Uzoma Uponi gained a reputation as a gifted storyteller when her debut novel, *ColourBLIND*, was a finalist at the Commonwealth Writers Prize. Her second novel, *Whispers from Yesteryears*, is a sequel to *ColourBLIND* and continues to inspire her readers. Through her stories, Uzoma lends her unique voice to the growing African narrative and introduces readers to some of the cultural beliefs that have shaped contemporary African lifestyles. Uzoma and her husband, Matthew, are parents to four children—David, Matthew-Daniel, Paul, and Michael—and make their home in Calgary.

CPSIA information can be obtained
at www.ICGtesting.com
Printed in the USA
BVHW071709291021
620254BV00001B/5